SERIES EDITOR: MARTIN WINDRO

ELITE 74

PRIVATEERS & PIRATES
1730–1830

TEXT BY
ANGUS KONSTAM

COLOUR PLATES BY
ANGUS McBRIDE

First published in 2001 by Osprey Publishing, Elms Court,
Chapel Way, Botley, Oxford OX2 9LP, United Kingdom
Email: **info@ospreypublishing.com**

ISBN 1 84176 016 1

Editor: Anita Hitchings
Design: Alan Hamp
Index: Alan Rutter
Originated by Magnet Harlequin, Uxbridge, UK
Printed in China through World Print Ltd

01 02 03 04 05 10 9 8 7 6 5 4 3 2 1

FOR A CATALOGUE OF ALL TITLES PUBLISHED BY OSPREY
MILITARY AND AVIATION PLEASE WRITE TO:

**The Marketing Manager, Osprey Publishing Ltd, PO Box 140,
Wellingborough, Northants NN8 4ZA, United Kingdom**
Email: **info@ospreydirect.co.uk**

**The Marketing Manager, Osprey Direct USA,
c/o Motorbooks International, PO Box 1,
Osceola, WI 54020-0001, USA**
Email: **info@ospreydirectusa.com**

www.ospreypublishing.com

Artist's Note

Readers may care to note that the original paintings from which the
colour plates in this book were prepared are available for private
sale. All reproduction copyright whatsoever is retained by the
Publisher. All enquiries should be addressed to:

Scorpio Gallery, PO Box 475, Hailsham, E. Sussex BN27 2SL UK

The publishers regret that they can enter into no correspondence on
this matter.

PRIVATEERS & PIRATES 1730–1830

INTRODUCTION

WITH THE DEMISE of the pirate scourge of the early 18th century, many sea captains took to privateering as a means of making money. This was a form of nationally-sponsored piracy which reached its peak during the late 18th and early 19th centuries. Although a world-wide phenomenon, privateering proved particularly popular in the waters of the Americas. Rivalry between European powers and the rise of independence movements among the nations of the New World provided ample opportunities for privateering captains.

Privateering had existed as a tool of maritime warfare since the Middle Ages. 'Letters of reprisal', which provided an official sanction to those seeking revenge through retaliatory attacks, were issued to ship owners who had suffered loss from vessels of an enemy country as early as the 14th century. A privateer is essentially someone who attacks the shipping of an enemy country during wartime with the approval of their own national government. This form of legitimised piracy proved extremely popular, and soon letters of reprisal or 'letters of marque' were issued to almost anyone who applied for them. At minimal cost a nation could attack the maritime commerce of an enemy without diverting the resources of its national fleet. For small maritime powers such as the United States of America during the American Revolution and the War of 1812, this proved a vital part of its maritime strategy.

The War of the Austrian Succession in 1739 placed Spanish maritime links with its New World colonies at risk from privateering attacks, and France in turn suffered a devastating period when trade with her island colonies in the West Indies was devastated. This disruption of maritime commerce proved so lucrative for British and American colonial ship owners that the resumption of hostilities between France and Britain in 1759 prompted an even greater wave of privateering. By the end of the Seven Years War in 1763, privateering was regarded as a vital element of maritime warfare, and Eastern Seaboard ports such as Halifax, Salem and Newport became thriving privateer bases.

When the American colonies rebelled against Britain in 1775, sea power was regarded as a dominant issue by both sides. Britain maintained the largest merchant fleet in the

The American privateer *Rattlesnake* portrayed under sail before her capture in 1781. Ship plans were produced by the Admiralty when she was bought into Royal Naval service, making her one of the few contemporary privateers whose specification has survived. Line drawing by Henry Rusk. (Author's collection)

world during the late 18th century, and the successful conclusion of the war in the colonies required its control over the Atlantic sea lanes. Similarly, the American economy was dependent on maritime trade, given the poor state of internal communications within the 13 colonies. A crippling British blockade of the American coastline could be expected, so many ship owners considered their only chance for economic survival was to turn to privateering. With no possibility of being able to match British naval strength, the colonies had to rely on European allies to contest British maritime dominance. All America could hope for was to cause sufficient losses in the British merchant fleet to force her merchants to put pressure on the government to end the conflict.

The French Revolutionary War and the Quasi-War between America and France both provided opportunities for privateers, but the failure of the French fleet to effectively challenge British control of sea power meant that by 1802, French prizes were rare. The French invasion of Spain in 1807 made the Spanish allies of the British, reducing privateering opportunities still further. The golden opportunity for ship owners on both sides of the Atlantic came in 1812, when Britain and America found themselves at war once again.

The War of 1812, which lasted until 1815, saw a resurgence of privateering, and by the end of 1812 the actions of hundreds of British, American and Canadian privateers began to take effect on maritime commerce. Ship owners launched purpose-built privateering vessels, and privateering reached its peak during the second year of the war. With over 500 American privateers at sea, the British instituted transatlantic convoys for protection, and by late 1814 a powerful naval blockade of the American coast kept the Americans in port. By the time peace was

Bonhomme Richard and Serapis, 23 September 1779. **Hand-coloured engraving, dated 1779. John Paul Jones' 42-gun warship is shown alongside the** *Serapis,* **supported by the gunfire of a consort. The reversed image is from a glass transfer print. (Hensley Collection, Ashville, NC)**

declared in 1815, British ship owners had lost over 1,000 merchant ships, and the American economy was in ruins. Peace brought a resurgence of maritime commerce, but the threat of privateers was replaced by the spectre of piracy. Privateering was used as a tool by the emerging Latin American nations, who were less able to regulate its use. Many Latin American privateers turned to piracy, and the 1810s and 1820s were marked by a struggle to make the waters of the Caribbean safe for commerce. The eradication of piracy in the Caribbean marked the end of centuries of conflict in American waters, where sea dogs, buccaneers, pirates and privateers had all contributed to the disruption of maritime trade.

Where possible, this survey of privateering in the Americas has drawn on original material — letters of marque, shipping records from ports such as Salem and Baltimore, reminiscences of privateering captains, and newspaper reports written during the last upsurge of piracy. What is apparent is that these records are often incomplete, as folios have been misplaced, returns were never submitted or there was little documentation to begin with. Some of the gaps in the narrative have been filled in by consulting a number of privateering histories, and the most readily available of these are listed in the bibliography. Of particular value were the archives and libraries of the Mariners' Museum in Newport News, Virginia, and the National Maritime Museum in Greenwich, London.

CHRONOLOGY

The War of the Austrian Succession, 1740–48 (Britain versus Spain and France)
1739	War of Jenkins' Ear provokes British conflict with Spain
1744	France allies with Spain
1748	Treaty of Aix-la-Chapelle ends conflict

The Seven Years War, 1755–63 (Britain versus France)
1755	undeclared war between Britain and France in the Americas, also known as the French and Indian war.
1757	Official declaration of war between France and Britain
1762	Spain allies with France
1763	Treaty of Paris ends conflict

The American Revolutionary War, 1775–83 (Britain versus the American colonies) *(also known as the American War of Independence)*
1775	The 13 American colonies rebel against British rule
1778	France allies with America
1779	Spain allies with America
1780	Holland allies with America
1783	Treaty of Versailles ends conflict

The French Revolutionary War, 1793–1802 (Britain versus France)
1793	Louis XVI executed, France declares war on Britain, Spain and Holland
1794	Holland, overrun by France, forms Batavian Republic (French ally)
1795	Treaty of Ildefenso – Spain makes peace, and allies with France
1802	Peace of Amiens ends conflict

The Quasi-War, 1798–1801 (France versus the United States)

1798   'Covert' war between France and United States

1801   President Jefferson ends conflict

The Napoleonic wars, 1803–15 (France and Spain versus Britain)

1803   Britain declares war with France

1804   Spain allies with France

1808   France invades Spain, Spain at war with France, and allied to Britain

1814   Treaty of Paris ends conflict

1815   Napoleon returns from exile, Britain and Holland declare war on France

            Peace following Napoleon's surrender to Royal Navy

The War of 1812, 1812–15 (Britain versus the United States)

1812   United States declares war on Britain

1815   Treaty of Ghent ends conflict

The Latin American Wars of Independence, 1808–30 (Spain versus her colonies)

1808   Spain and Portugal invaded by France.

1809   Insurrection against Spanish rule in most of South America

1811–19 Independence granted to Paraguay (1811), Argentina (1816), Chile (1818) and Colombia (1819)

1822   Ecuador and Brazil (a Portuguese colony) become independent

1823   United provinces (much of Central America) become independent (dissolved in 1839)

1824   Peru and Mexico independent

1825–28 Bolivia (1825), Uruguay (1828) and Venezuela (1830) become independent

(Note: civil wars and disputes continued throughout South America during this period.)

Boscawen and Sheerness Privateers, 3 July 1745. Hand-coloured engraving, dated 1753. The frigate HMS *Boscawen* supported by English privateers attacked a small French convoy returning from the West Indies, and captured or sank six of the eight French merchant vessels present. (Hensley Collection, Ashville, NC)

THE DEVELOPMENT OF PRIVATEERING

Colonial Roots

Traditionally, conflicts between European powers were reflected by the extension of the war to include their American colonies. War between France and England during the War of the League of Augsburg (1690–97) and the War of the Spanish Succession (1701–13) had few repercussions in North America. The involvement of Spain in both these conflicts laid her open to attacks by the French and then the English. The English colonies (or British from 1707) were too preoccupied with the threat of Indian raids on land and piratical attacks at sea to consider the disruption of their fragile economy or to conduct widespread privateering. Instead, British privateers established bases in the colonies and in the West Indies, and prosecuted their own attacks on the French and Spanish.

Privateering in American waters became established with the War of Jenkins' Ear in 1739 (which preceded Britain's entrance into the war of the Austrian Succession, 1740–48) when colonial privateers were fitted out for attacks against the Spanish. When France entered the conflict in 1744, American privateers began operating in the Gulf of St Lawrence and off the French islands of the West Indies, while French Canadian privateers cruised off New England. Privateers assisted the British army to transport troops to attack the French fortress of Louisburg in 1745, and their independent cruises began to demonstrate the effectiveness of privateering. In June 1744 two New York privateers captured a French prize valued at over £11,000, while the following year the 20-gun privateer *Shirley* captured eight French vessels in Canadian waters. In 1746 New York privateers captured several valuable French prizes, and the New York courts record the division of cargoes of indigo (a valuable blue dye), sugar, coffee and cotton; the produce of the French Caribbean provinces. That summer the privateers *Greyhound* and *Dragon* captured a Spanish privateering vessel, so attacks were not limited to French shipping. One New York paper records a Danish ship being stopped by a New York-based privateer, and Spanish passengers forced to hand over their possessions. As Denmark was neutral, the Danish captain was paid for his trouble and allowed to proceed. Although this clearly overstepped the line between privateering and piracy, the perpetrator, one Captain Troup, was never prosecuted.

The start of the Seven Years War provided similar opportunities for the American colonists, although French Canadian privateers preyed on New England shipping in retaliation. Although the conquest of New France (Canada) ended privateering activities for a time, fresh opportunities arose when Spain entered the conflict in 1762.

Phoenix and Rose, 16 August 1776. Hand-coloured engraving, dated 1778. Depiction of the attack by privateersmen and regular sailors on British warships in the Hudson River. (Hensley Collection, Ashville, NC)

For the next two years, ports such as New York, Boston and Charleston all recorded the capture of Spanish prizes.

The American Revolution

The heyday of privateering in the Americas followed the revolt of Britain's American colonies, and lasted intermittently until 1814. A few statistics demonstrate the importance of privateering to the American revolutionary cause. Congress commissioned less than 50 warships during the revolt, and they were almost exclusively employed as commerce raiders, capturing 196 British vessels. During the war 792 letters of marque were issued, and these privateers captured in excess of 600 British merchant ships, with an estimated total value of $18 million in contemporary value. Of even greater importance, the privateers captured around 16,000 British seamen, at a time when the Royal Navy was desperately short of men and ships. Losses also included troops, munitions and military equipment vitally needed in the American theatre. Although individually insignificant, losses such as the 240 Hessian troops captured by the privateer *Mars,* or the 100 British soldiers captured by the privateer *Warren* accrued to form a significant drain on British resources. Post-revolutionary American propaganda claims the capture of over 16,000 military prisoners by the Navy and privateers, but modern scholarly assessments place the figure at less than 2,000; still a significant loss when for most of the southern campaign of 1780–81, Cornwallis had a field army of less than 2,000 men.

The colonists had no purpose-built privateers when the war started, and no regular navy. Initial attacks were conducted using hastily adapted

American Merchant Ship Planter, 10 July 1799. **Hand-coloured engraving, dated 1800. The** *Planter* **fought off the 22-gun French privateer in a protracted engagement. The French privateer is shown flying both a French national colour and an all-red privateer flag. (Hensley Collection, Ashville, NC)**

merchant vessels, and small inshore rowing craft known as 'spider catchers', a form of improvised coastal gunboat. The Americans had a number of ports which specialised in building vessels well suited to privateering; small, fast-hulled topsail schooners, which were easily adapted with the addition of guns and crewmen. The first prizes were captured in the summer of 1775, and by the winter of 1775–76, American privateers had become a serious nuisance in the waters of New England and the middle colonies. From November 1775 until April 1776, 31 British or loyalist ships were captured off Boston, and these attacks helped induce the British to withdraw from the port in March. Similarly, the Royal Navy captured several privateers during the same period, carrying them into Boston as prizes.

With colonial merchant trading virtually at a standstill, many American ports turned to privateering as a means to make a living. As the first wave of converted merchant vessels, whalers and fishing boats were captured by Royal Navy patrols, ship owners began to launch purpose-built privateers, and increasing numbers of letters of marque were signed by Congress or by state authorities. In two years from the summer of 1775, the following privateering licences were granted (listed by state, and principal port):

State	Licences	Port
Massachusetts	53	(Boston, Salem, Marblehead, Gloucester, Portland, New Bedford)
New Hampshire	7	(Portsmouth)
Rhode Island	6	(Providence)
Connecticut	22	(Bridgeport, New Haven, New London)
New York	7	(New York)
New Jersey	1	(New Brunswick)
Pennsylvania	21	(Philadelphia)
Delaware	0	
Maryland	6	(Baltimore, Annapolis)
Virginia	0	
North Carolina	3	(Wilmington)
South Carolina	6	(Charleston)
Georgia	0	

The British occupation of Rhode Island, New York and parts of New Jersey limited privateering activity in those states, while in the south, a lack of suitable vessels and the proximity of British squadrons made extensive privateering impractical. Loyalists (or Tories) also fitted out privateers, principally based in New York and Newport, Rhode Island.

Privateering continued to provide a popular source of income for these colonial ports, but shipping losses led to a brief decrease in numbers before specially-built privateers became active. During 1777, only 73 American privateers were registered, but the numbers increased steadily until 1782, when many vessels were converted to merchant ships:

1778	115 vessels
1779	167 vessels
1780	228 vessels
1781	449 vessels
1782	323 vessels

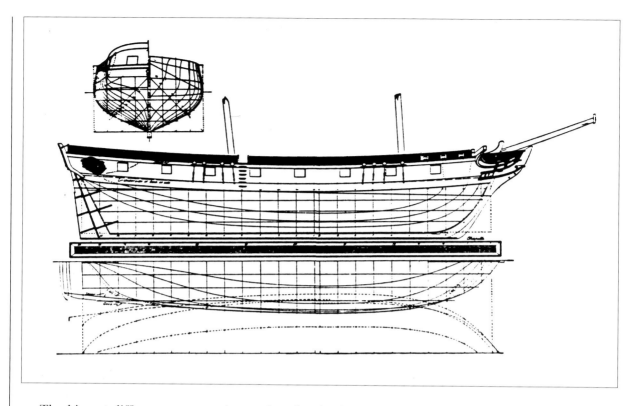

The biggest difference was not in numbers but in the size of vessel. While the first wave of privateers were converted from small merchant vessels and carried less than ten guns, by 1779 large privateers carrying over 20 guns were common, and many were capable of cruising in the mid-Atlantic or in British waters. Vessels such as the *General Washington* or the *General Pickering* were considered the most powerful American ships afloat, given the almost complete demise of the Continental Navy. The Royal Navy would have diverted resources to counter the activities of privateers (as she did so successfully in the War of 1812), but the involvement of France, Spain and Holland stretched the British to the limit. There were simply no ships to spare for a blockade of American ports. The adoption of convoy systems limited but failed to prevent losses to privateers, and by the early 1780s, merchants were lobbying the government to bring an end to the war. By disregarding the threat of privateering until it was too late to control, the British sealed their own fate in the Americas. While the intervention of other European powers on America's behalf turned the course of the rebellion in America's favour, the economic warfare wrought by the privateers made the outcome inevitable.

The War of 1812

Although an unpopular conflict with many Americans, the War of 1812 initially provided a great opportunity for the ship owners of the United States and to a lesser extent, Canada. British naval power was stretched thinly because of the demands of the Napoleonic War. A series of trade embargoes and import laws, coupled with a European blockade, had reduced the commercial profits available to many American merchants,

The US schooner of war *Vixen*, launched in 1803, carried 14 guns, and became the first of a series of small warships designed to protect commerce from attacks by enemy privateers. Around 1810 these schooners were reconfigured as brigs, allowing a heavier armament to be carried, but sacrificing the speed they needed to fulfil their role. (Mel Fisher Maritime Museum, Key West, Florida)

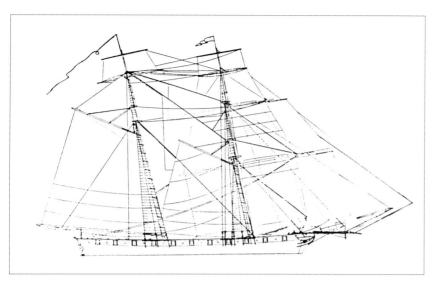

The sail plan of the American privateering schooner *Prince de Neufchâtel* in 1813. In October 1814 while under the command of the French-born Captain Ordronaux her crew repulsed a boarding attempt by ship's boats from HMS *Endymion*. (Mel Fisher Maritime Museum, Key West, Florida)

so the opportunity of widespread privateering was welcomed as an alternative to commercial trading.

War was declared by President Madison in June, and the small United States Navy scrambled to face a conflict it was not prepared for. Privateers were seen as a vital part of naval policy, and letters of marque were issued almost immediately. From the onset of the war until its end in January 1815, 517 privateering licences were granted by the president, and over 1,300 prizes were taken, the majority within the first ten months of the conflict.

The effects of such heavy losses were pronounced. British newspapers recounted the damage done to the maritime economy, and in Liverpool, a master of a British merchant ship who had already been captured three times before the war, described how he saw ten American privateers during his voyage over from Nova Scotia. By late 1813, insurance companies refused to insure any vessel bound for Halifax, Nova Scotia, and premiums for other destinations had increased by between 25 and 50 per cent.

The British were not the only nation to suffer. Forty-one privateering licences were issued in New Brunswick and Nova Scotia during the war, and these Canadian privateers preyed on the coastal shipping of New England. To many Canadian ship owners, privateering was a less attractive option than commercial trade, as her merchants still

The 20-gun *America* was one of the most successful privateers of the War of 1812, taking 26 prizes during the conflict. She was owned by the Crowninshield family of Salem, Massachusetts, a family who made a fortune from privateering. (Private collection)

maintained a brisk business with Britain and her colonies in the West Indies, so there was still a less risky alternative. Despite this, Halifax and Liverpool, Nova Scotia, bustled with privateering activity, and one Canadian vessel, the *Liverpool Packet*, captured 50 American prizes alone. From late 1813, British privateers began to operate in American waters, and newspapers printed in the English ports of Liverpool and Plymouth soon reported the sale of American prizes and their cargo. The waters around Cape Cod became almost too dangerous for American ships to enter by the spring of 1813.

By the end of 1813, the privateering heyday was over. A British naval blockade was established along the American Atlantic seaboard during the winter of 1813–14, and although numerous American privateers continued to operate from ports in France, the Caribbean or South America, the numbers fell sharply, so that by the summer of 1814, insurance rates had almost returned to pre-war levels. Canadian and British privateers were converted back into merchant ships, and denied the income from prizes, and American privateering ports such as Salem, Boston, Newport, New York and Baltimore all suffered economic ruin. The blockade effectively halted American trade, and the same ship owners who had welcomed the war as an opportunity to profit from privateering, now clamoured for peace. Peace commissioners met in Belgium, and in January 1815 the futile war was brought to a close. Former privateersmen returned to their peacetime pursuits, and although Latin American countries continued to use privateers in their independence struggles with Spain, privateering ceased to be a legitimate occupation. Apart from an outbreak of piracy in the Caribbean, American vessels were free to trade wherever they wished, and the decades following 1815 saw a boom in American maritime trade. For Americans, privateering was no longer an option, and there was simply too much legitimate activity to make the risks of piracy appealing.

Hinchbrook and Privateer Grand Turk, 1 May 1814. **Coloured aquatint engraving, dated 1819. The 18-gun** *Grand Turk* **of Salem captured 30 British vessels during the War of 1812, but in this engagement the British Postal Packet fought off the American privateer. (Hensley Collection, Ashville, NC)**

Certainly pirates such as Jean Laffite existed, and a number of former American privateersmen turned to piratical activities in areas outside the reach of the authorities. For the vast majority of mariners and ship owners, the trading opportunities presented by a world at peace filled the economic niche once offered by privateering.

One valuable benefit of the privateering experiences of both the American Revolution and the War of 1812 was the development of ships designed from the hull up as large, fast privateers. Vessels such as the *Prince de Neufchâtel* or the *General Armstrong* of New York were a new class of 'super privateers', and together with the converted Baltimore schooners, they assisted in the evolutionary process which produced the fast slaving ships or the schooners of the post-war years, and eventually developed into the design known as the clipper ship.

The last pirates

Both the Anglo-American war of 1812 and the Napoleonic wars ended in 1815. Privateering was in its zenith, and although most mariners returned to legitimate employment, several did not. Some sought service as privateers working on behalf of the new Latin American states, while others simply operated outside the law, turning to piracy. For 15 years a new wave of attacks swept through the American seaboard and the Caribbean. It was the worst outbreak of lawlessness on the high seas for a century.

Although some of these pirates, such as Jean Laffite, were American, the majority came from Latin America. When France invaded Spain in 1808, many Latin Americans took advantage of the Spanish preoccupation with affairs at home and rebelled against their colonial masters. Rebel governments such as those of Venezuela and Colombia handed out hundreds of privateering contracts to anyone willing to attack Spanish shipping. Many of these privateers were unwilling to restrict their attacks to Spanish vessels, and by 1820 vessels of all nationalities entered the waters of the Caribbean at their peril. These piratical attacks were finally ended by aggressive naval action by Britain and the United States.

Victims for these latter-day pirates were easily found. Following the end of the Napoleonic wars, merchant shipping tried to fulfil the

Isometric reconstruction of a US naval brig of war of the *Vixen* class, *c.* 1812. Although the *Nautilus* and *Vixen* were captured by the Royal Navy during the War of 1812, their half-sister, USS *Enterprise,* went on to lead the first anti-piracy squadron in the Gulf of Mexico in the 1820s. (Mel Fisher Maritime Museum, Key West, Florida)

increasing demand for trade goods and raw materials, and booming European and American economies provided ready markets on both sides of the Atlantic. The numbers of merchant vessels in operation doubled over a ten-year period, meaning that the shipping lanes of the world were busier than at any other time in history. The demand for rum, sugar, spices, slaves, timber and other commodities

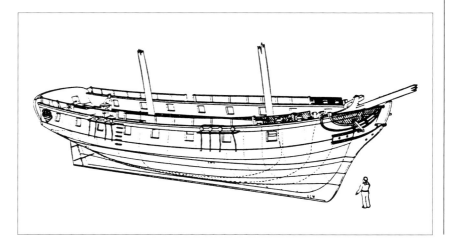

The American ship-sloop USS *Peacock* as she appeared soon after her launch in 1813. A sister-ship of the sloops *Wasp* and *Frolic*, *Peacock* was designed as a commerce raider and survived the war. She served as a pirate-hunter during the early 1820s. Line drawing by Henry Rusk. (Author's collection)

meant that the waters of the Caribbean and the Gulf of Mexico were used by thousands of vessels, and areas such as the Florida Straits, the Bahamas Channel and the Windward Passage became some of the busiest shipping lanes in the Americas.

Many of the pirates who preyed on these ships were opportunists, simply attacking vulnerable ships if the opportunity presented itself. Others were more methodical, preying on certain types of vessels such as slave ships with a view to selling the cargo to fulfil a demand by merchants in league with the pirates. American shipping was particularly badly hit. Maritime insurance rates soared between 1815 and 1820, and eventually many companies refused to underwrite vessels sailing into Caribbean waters. From 1820, the American and British navies diverted resources to combat piracy in the region, regardless of the political or diplomatic consequences. A combination of aggressive patrolling and attacks on pirate bases eventually forced most surviving pirates to abandon their attacks, and by 1826 this last wave of piracy had been contained.

A handful of particularly brutal pirates still remained at large into the 1830s, but one by one they were caught and executed, and by 1840, piracy was considered a thing of the past in American or Atlantic waters. These last cut-throats included the Portuguese pirate Benito de Soto (*c.* 1828–29) and Pedro Gibert (*c.* 1832–33), and their attacks provided the newspapers with suitably shocking copy. Their capture marked the end of almost 400 years of piracy, buccaneering and privateering in American waters, although it has been argued that the Confederate raiders followed in the footsteps of these earlier cut-throats, and the Northern press during the American Civil War (1861–65) referred to these maritime raiders as pirates.

ORGANISATION AND RECRUITMENT

Privateering contracts

The practice of privateering was well defined in the late 18th century, with British, French and American privateers following similar internationally recognised procedures. The application and award of a letter of marque (or 'letter of reprisal'), the procedure involved in taking a prize and the subsequent adjudication of the sale of the vessel and cargo, followed a similar pattern in Liverpool, Dunkirk or Boston. When war was declared, the government passed a General Prize Act or similar form of legislation, effectively legitimising privateering. It could then issue privateering commissions (letters of marque). An application was made for a privateering commission by the captain of a privateering vessel, either individually, or in conjunction with a consortium of ship owners. In Britain or France, the application was made to the Admiralty, and in America, letters of marque were initially issued by state governors. From April 1776, the Continental Congress issued privateering commissions, and state commissions were discarded in July 1780. The letter of marque ensured that in time of war, the privateer was entitled to his prize and, at least in theory, was safe from prosecution. The official sanction of a government was vital, as without it, captured privateersmen could be tried and hanged as pirates. The letter stated the names of the ship's owners (and their town of origin), the names of the captain and

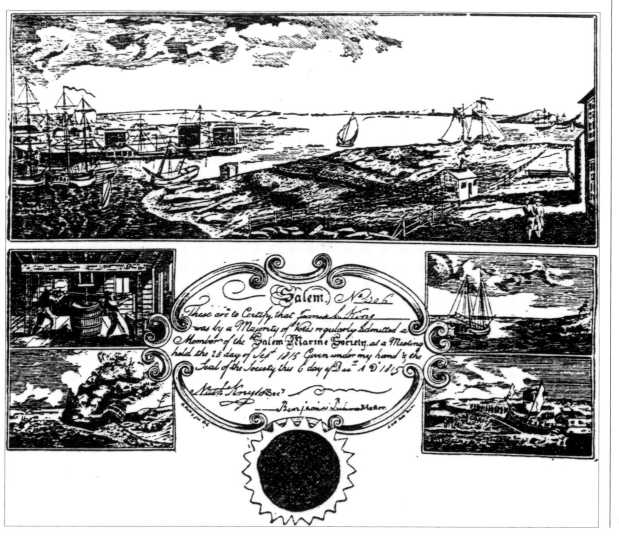

A Certificate of Membership of Salem Marine Society, dated December 1815. It shows a general view of Crowinshield Wharf in Salem, and the launch of the privateer *Fame* in 1812, one of 40 based in the port during the War of 1812. (Private collection)

senior officers and described the vessel's name, tonnage, crew size and armament, making the documents uniquely tailored to a particular ship and her crew. Similarly, a letter only gave official sanction to attack the shipping of one particular country. If the war expanded to include fresh enemies, separate letters of marque had to be granted to cover the new belligerents. An example of the wording from an American letter of marque dated 1812 included the phrase: 'This commission to continue in force during the pleasure of the President of the United States for the time being'. In other words, as soon as the president made peace with the enemy, the document was invalid.

In addition to the application for the letter, the government almost always established rules under which privateers were required to operate. Ship owners or investors were usually required to post a bond with the government to guarantee the good behaviour of the privateering crew. In 1812 this was set at between $5,000 and $10,000 in the United States, or between £1,500 and £3,000 in Britain or Canada, depending on the size of vessel and crew. At the start of the American Revolution, a bond was required from both Congress and the individual state, but this was streamlined in 1780 when the states withdrew from sanctioning privateers. A sworn affidavit from the backers agreed to government control over their activities. The following example of the 'Instructions' supplied when a letter of marque was issued by Congress in 1776 are typical of the restrictions imposed by most privateering nations during the period.

Copy of a privateering letter of marque issued in 1800 on behalf of the President of the United States of America. It entitled Captain Nathaniel Silsbee and the ten-gun privateer *Herald* to 'seize and take any armed French vessel'. (Private collection)

IN CONGRESS
WEDNESDAY, APRIL 3, 1776

INSTRUCTIONS to the COMMANDERS of Private Ships or Vessels of War, which shall have Commissions or Letters of Marque and Reprisal, authorising them to make Captures of British Vessels and Cargoes.

I.

YOU may, by Force of Arms, attack, subdue, and take all ships and other Vessels belonging to the Inhabitants of Great-Britain, on the High Seas, between high-water and low-water marks, except Ships and Vessels bringing Persons who intend to settle and reside in the United Colonies, or bringing Arms, Ammunition and War-like Stores to the said Colonies, for the use of such Inhabitants thereof that are Friends to the American Cause, which you shall suffer to pass unmolested, the Commanders thereof permitting a peaceable Search, and giving satisfactory Information of the Contents of the Landings, and Destination of the Voyages.

II.

You may, by Force of Arms, attack, subdue, and take all Ships and their Vessels whatsoever carrying Soldiers, Arms, Gun-powder, Ammunition,

Provisions, or any other contraband Goods, to any of the British Armies or Ships of War employed against these Colonies.

III.

You shall bring such Ships and Vessels you shall take, with their Guns, Rigging, Tackle, Apparel, Furniture and Landings to some convenient Port or Ports of the United Colonies, that Proceedings may thereupon be had in due Form before the Courts which are or shall be there appointed to hear and determine Causes civil and maritime.

IV.

You or one of your Chief Officers shall bring or send the master and Pilot and one or more principal Person or persons of the Company of every Ship or Vessel by you taken, as soon after the Capture as may be, to the Judge or Judges of such Court aforesaid, to be examined upon Oath, and make Answer to the Interrogatories which may be propounded touching the Interest or property of the Ship or Vessel, and her Lading; and at the same Time you shall deliver or cause to be delivered to the Judge or Judges, all Passes, Sea-Briefs, Charter-Parties, Bills of lading, Dockets, Letters, and other Documents and Writings found on Board, proving the said Papers by the Affidavit of yourself, or some other Person present at the Capture, to be produced as they were received, without Fraud, Addition, Subduction or Embezzlement.

V.

You shall keep and preserve every Ship or Vessel and Cargo by you taken, until they shall by Sentence of a Court properly authorised be adjudged lawful Prize, not selling, spoiling, wasting or diminishing the same, or breaking the Bulk thereof, nor suffering any such Thing to be done.

VI.

If you, or any of your Officers and Crew shall, in cold Blood, kill or maim, or, by Torture or otherwise, cruelly, inhumanely, and contrary to common Usage and the Practice of civilized nations in War, treat any person or persons surprized in the Ship or Vessel you shall take, the Offender shall be severely punished.

VII.

You shall, by all convenient Opportunities, send to Congress written Accounts of the Captures you shall make, with the Number and names of the Captives, Copies of your Journal from Time to Time, and Intelligence of what may occur or be discovered concerning the Designs of the Enemy, and the Destination, Motions and Operations of their Fleets and Armies.

VIII.

One Third, at the least, of your whole Company shall be land-Men.

IX.

You shall not ransome any Prisoners or Captives, but shall dispose of them in such Manner as the Congress, or if that be not fitting in the Colony whither they shall be brought, as the General Assembly, Convention, or Council or Committee of Safety of such Colony shall direct.

X.

You shall observe all such further Instructions as Congress shall hereafter give in the premises, when you shall have Notice thereof.

XI.

If you shall do any Thing contrary to the Instructions, or to others hereafter to be given, or willingly suffer such Thing to be done, you shall not only forfeit your Commission, and be liable to an Action for Breach of the Condition of your Bond, but be responsible to the party grieved for damages sustained by such Mal-versation.

By Order of Congress,

John Hancock PRESIDENT

The issue of letters of marque and 'instructions' were vital parts of the waging of maritime war by the late 18th century, and the system was recognised throughout the maritime world. It was also vital to start issuing them as soon as possible after war was declared, in order to catch enemy shipping before they could start arming themselves. During the War of 1812, Britain (and Canada) held off making a formal declaration of war for several months, so privateering was slow in receiving official approval. During the same time, although the United States navy was ill-prepared for the conflict, Congress had the administration required to grant privateering licences already in place. This meant that letters of marque were being issued within weeks of the president's declaration. It also bears testimony to the international nature of privateering that although thousands of vessels, both Britain and American, were captured by privateers during the War of 1812, only a handful of official complaints were made by the victims against their privateering captors. The bonding system and the strict rules governing the distribution of the captured ship and cargo were sufficient to prevent most transgressions of maritime law.

A recruiting poster produced by John Paul Jones in an attempt to recruit sailors and landsmen for his command, the 20-gun corvette USS *Ranger*. Recruiting for the Navy was a problem given that privateering was considered far more lucrative. (Naval Historical Foundation)

Recruitment

Before a letter of marque could be issued, the ship owners or investors who backed the venture had to appoint a captain and also at least two of his senior officers; the first lieutenant (or 'master') and his next-in-command (the second lieutenant or 'mate'). These ship's officers would be selected through reputation as sea captains, or occasionally appointed because of family connection or because of their own financial investment in the privateering venture. Few of these men were formally educated, but all shared a similar background of maritime experience. It was not in the owner's interests to appoint captains who did not have the experience needed to undertake the challenging tasks required of them, or to have men who lacked the respect of the crew.

Once a vessel was selected and the captain and officers appointed, the next task was to find a crew. In theory this was a simple process, as most seamen were hired from the home port of the privateering vessel. After a period of warfare, naval recruitment (or the activities of press-gangs) and the sheer number of

GREAT
ENCOURAGEMENT
FOR
SEAMEN.

ALL GENTLEMEN SEAMEN and able-bodied LANDSMEN who have a Mind to distinguish themselves in the GLORIOUS CAUSE of their COUNTRY, and make their Fortunes, an Opportunity now offers on board the Ship RANGER, of Twenty Guns, (for FRANCE) now laying in PORTSMOUTH, in the State of NEW-HAMPSHIRE, commanded by JOHN PAUL JONES Esq; let them repair to the Ship's Rendezvous in PORTSMOUTH, or at the Sign of Commodore MANLEY, in SALEM, where they will be kindly entertained, and receive the greatest Encouragement.---The Ship RANGER, in the Opinion of every Person who has seen her is looked upon to be one of the best Cruizers in America.---She will be always able to Fight her Guns under a most excellent Cover ; and no Vessel yet built was ever calculated for sailing faster, and making good Weather.

Any Gentlemen VOLUNTEERS who have a Mind to take an agreable Voyage in this pleasant Season of the Year, may, by entering on board the above Ship RANGER, meet with every Civility they can possibly expect, and for a further Encouragement depend on the first Opportunity being embraced to reward each one agreable to his Merit.

All reasonable Travelling Expences will be allowed, and the Advance-Money be paid on their Appearance on Board.

In CONGRESS, MARCH 29, 1777.

RESOLVED,

THAT the MARINE COMMITTEE be authorised to advance to every able Seaman, that enters into the CONTINENTAL SERVICE, any Sum not exceeding FORTY DOLLARS, and to every ordinary Seaman or Landsman, any Sum not exceeding TWENTY DOLLARS, to be deducted from their future Prize-Money.

By Order of CONGRESS,
JOHN-HANCOCK, PRESIDENT.

DANVERS: Printed by E. RUSSELL, at the House late the Bell-Tavern.

privateering vessels at sea meant that suitable seamen were hard to find. Most privateering instructions specified the hiring of a certain percentage of 'landsmen' – men with no previous maritime experience, a device used to expand the available pool of labour. The crew were usually recruited for a specific duration, or for a single voyage, and paid off when the ship returned to port. Obviously, the more successful the privateering captain and vessel, the easier it would be to find a crew. Advertisements were posted in taverns and in local newspapers, such as this example from the *Boston Gazette* of November 1780:

For SALE by the CANDLE,

AT the Loudon Tavern, Foxhole-street, Plymouth, on Wednesday the 9th of May, 1781, at Ten o'Clock in the Forenoon precisely,
The Good Ship TWEE GEBROEDERS, Dutch built, round stern'd, Burthen 600 Tons, more or less, almost New, and is a real good Ship, well found in Stores, and is fit for the East Country, or Norway Trade, a Dutch Prize, taken on her Passage from Alicant to Amsterdam, by the British Lion Private Ship of War, Arthur French, Esq. Commander, now lying at Plymouth, and there to be delivered.
Inventories will be timely delivered on Board, at the Place of Sale, or by applying at the Broker's Office, on the New Quay, Plymouth.

PETER SYMONS, Sworn Broker.

'An Invitation to all brave Seamen and Marines, who have an inclination to serve their country and make their Fortunes. The grand Privateer Ship DEANE, commanded by Elisha Hinman Esq., and prov'd to be a very capital sailor, will sail on a cruise against the enemies of the United States of America, by the 20th instant. The DEANE mounts thirty carriage guns, and is excellently well calculated for Attacks, Defence and Pursute. This therefore is to invite all those Jolly Fellows who love their Country, and want to make their Fortunes at One Stroke, to repair immediately to the Rendezvous at the Head of His Excellency Governor Hancock's Wharf, where they will be received with a hearty welcome by a number of Brave Fellows there assembled, and treated with what excellent Liquor call'd Grog which is allow'd by all true Seamen to be the Liquor of Life.'

The American Revolution became a far more widespread conflict from 1778, and by early 1781, English privateers were licensed to attack French, Spanish and Dutch shipping. Advertisement from the *Exeter Flying Post*, April 1781. (Author's collection)

Once these volunteers arrived, the captain would select the most promising or experienced men, including the required quota of landsmen, or 'landlubbers'. Compared to the navy, privateering offered the opportunity of short voyages, less severe discipline and far greater financial reward. While the Royal Navy had to resort to the use of 'press-gangs' to crew its ships, privateers had their pick of crew, especially as once on the books, they were largely exempt from the press. The sailors in regular merchant service were not so fortunate, and often service aboard a privateer became the only safe haven if empressment into the navy was to be avoided. The only real drawback was that the privateersmen received no regular wages; they were paid only when they successfully captured a prize.

This reward came in the form of shares, and the method of apportioning them was laid down in the Ship's Articles, signed by everyone on board when they joined. The Articles also stipulated that the captain and his officers abide by the 'Instructions' laid down by the government issuing the letter of marque, and that before the apportion of share money following the legal sale of the prize ship and her contents, the owners and financial backers would get their own return. The standard for this was that the backers divided 50 per cent of the value of each prize between them, leaving the rest of the value to be apportioned between the crew in accordance with the Articles. An example of the Articles from a Salem privateer of 1780 shows how this worked (see overleaf).

Example of Articles from a Salem privateer of 1780

Rewards and Punishment

1. Any of the company losing an arm or a leg in an engagement, or is otherwise disabled and unable to earn his bread, shall receive £1,000 from the first prize taken.

2. Whoever first discovers a sail that proves to be a prize, shall receive £100 as a reward for his vigilance.

3. Whoever enters an enemy ship after boarding orders are issued, shall receive £300 for his valour.

4. Whoever is guilty of gaming or quarrelling shall suffer such punishment as the Captain and Officers see fit.

5. Any man absent from the ship for 24 hours without leave shall be guilty of disobedience. Whoever is guilty of cowardice, mutiny, theft, pilfering, embezzlement, concealment of goods belonging to the ship or her company, stripping or threatening any man or behaving indecently to a woman shall loose his shares and receive such other punishment as the crime deserves. Such forfeited shares shall be distributed to the remaining ship's company.

6. Seven dead shares shall be set aside by the Captain and Officers among those who behave best, and do most for the interest and service of the cruise. The Captain, Lieutenants, Master, Surgeon and Officer of the Marines shall not be entitled to any part of the dead shares.

7. When a prize is taken and sent into port, the Prize Master and the men aboard are responsible for watching and unloading the prize. If any negligence results in damage, their shares will be held accountable.

8. If the Commander is disabled, the next highest officer will strictly comply with the rules, orders, restrictions and agreements between the owners of the privateer and the commander.

9. If any Officer or any of the company is taken prisoner aboard a captured prize vessel, he shall receive a share in all prizes taken during the remainder of the cruise, as he would if actually aboard. However, he must obtain his liberty before the end of the cruise or make every effort to join the privateer, or else his prize money is forfeited to the owners and the ship's company.

10. The Captain shall have full power to displace any officer who may be found unfit for the post.

11. The Captain and his principal officers shall have full power to appoint an Agent for the ship's company.

12. Shares are to be apportioned as follows:

Captain:	8 shares
First Lieutenant, Second Lieutenant, Master, Surgeon:	4 shares
Officer of Marines, Prize Master, Carpenter, Gunner, Boatswain, Master's Mate, Captain's Clerk, Steward:	2 shares
Sailmaker, Armourer, Sergeant of Marines, Cook, Gunner's Mate, Boatswain's Mate, Carpenter's Mate, Surgeon's Mate, Cooper:	1½ shares
Gentlemen Volunteer, Seaman:	1 share
Boy under 16 years:	½ share

Captain John Carnes, a privateering captain from Salem, Massachusetts, during the American Revolution. The Carnes family were also prominent shipowners, and together with the Derby and Crowninshield families, formed part of the 'privateering gentry' who profited considerably from the conflict. Illustration by C. Keith Wilbur. (Stackpole Books)

Privateering crews

It has already been noted that privateers rarely had a problem recruiting crewmen. At least two out of every three sailors was an experienced seaman, either from a naval or mercantile background. The principal privateering ports of America, Britain and France were all bustling maritime centres, and the sailors and fishermen that inhabited them were for the most part well suited for the requirements of the privateer captains. In some cases, as a war progressed, captured seamen volunteered to join the crew of a privateer, and recruitment was not limited to seamen from the nation under whose flag the privateer was operating. An American privateer captured in 1814 by a Royal Navy frigate reportedly included British, French, Canadian, Dutch and Swedish seamen among her American crew.

Another group were landsmen, and most 'Instructions' specified that the crew must contain an agreed percentage of these inexperienced volunteers. For the most part they were required to learn the skills of their new profession as rapidly as possible, but as privateering cruises were so short and the ships so well manned, they were spared many of the more skilled tasks asked of the professional seamen. These landsmen came into their own during a boarding action, and as many were recruited from ex-soldiers or marines, they proved their worth in combat. A further group were the 'gentlemen volunteers', often the offspring of the ship owners or ship's officers. Unlike midshipmen in regular naval service, there was no requirement to train these young men to become officers, although that was certainly a widespread practice. Instead, they often acted as a marine guard, maintaining order

Privateers depicted by Frank Schoonover for the children's story *Privateers of '76* by Ralph D. Paine, which appeared in *American Boy Magazine*, July 1923. Although a dramatic representation, the figures are dressed appropriately. (Mariner's Museum, Newport News, Virginia)

Pirates clearing the decks of an East Indiaman. This early 19th-century British depiction of pirates includes references to the privateering activities of Robert Surcouf. Clearly the victims of privateering attacks saw little to differentiate between the two types of aggressors. (Mel Fisher Maritime Museum, Key West, Florida)

Captain Nathaniel Silsbee commanded the privateer *Herald* of Salem, Massachusetts, during the Quasi-War with France. Ironically, in 1800 he rescued the British merchant vessel *Cornwallis* from a French privateer in the Indian Ocean. (Author's collection)

within the ship and serving as leaders of boarding parties or sharp-shooters when in action. The more experienced gentlemen formed a pool from which 'prize masters' were drawn, although the command of prize ships could equally be given to an experienced mate. Promotion was rare during a cruise, but good performance was rewarded, and skilled mates or gentlemen volunteers were often considered suitable candidates for ships' officers once they had gained enough experience.

Being a sailor was a young man's profession. Statistical studies have shown that the average privateersman was in his 20s, and few were older than 40. The physical stamina and exertion required of a sailor during the period, combined with the often dangerous and unhealthy conditions, meant that older men were often not up to the task.

The dress of a privateering crew was typical of that of other sailors of the period. No uniforms were worn, but certain adaptations were made to clothes that were usually found on land. Pantaloons or 'petticoat breeches' were common, usually cut from white canvas. These were usually cut to reach above the ankle, and if shoes or stockings were worn, they were clearly visible below the breeches. These trousers developed into the more modern style of bell-bottomed white duck trousers by the early 19th century. Both were held up by leather belts. Plain cotton shirts were common, either with or without a collar, and secured by buttons or a drawstring. From the 1760s, woollen knitted shirts resembling a modern long-sleeved T-shirt were worn, often adorned with horizontal coloured bands. In cold weather a 'sailor's coat' or 'pea coat' was worn, usually made from blue canvas or wool impregnated with tar. A cloth neckerchief, or 'sweat rag' was also commonly worn according to contemporary illustrations. Headgear included regular cocked or tricorne hats, wide-brimmed round hats, slouch hats made from canvas or knitted woollen caps. Privateering officers often wore coats resembling the uniforms of the regular navy – long blue woollen coats with naval-style buttons and wide lapels. Contemporary paintings show that waistcoats and naval-style white breeches were also common, but certainly practical considerations would have outweighed almost all dress requirements for both officers and men.

THE PRIVATEERING ART OF WAR

The prey

After the first weeks of a war, unarmed enemy merchant ships sailing alone had either been captured or reached the safety of a friendly port. Merchant captains armed their ships before sending them to sea again, and clamoured to insure their vessel and cargo. Gun founding records from the iron industries in the Weald (Sussex and Kent) record a boom in trade at the start of all the conflicts of the 18th and early 19th centuries. Similarly, as shipping losses mounted, insurance companies stipulated the need for increased armament on all ships.

Within a few months, most unarmed enemy merchant vessels could only be found in waters they considered safe (usually their own coastal waters), or else they travelled in convoys. Some faster vessels opted to avoid the delays of waiting for a convoy to sail and relied on speed to avoid enemy privateers. Convoys were large, slow-moving affairs, and many ship owners felt that operating independently was worth the increased risk of being attacked by privateers. Often these fast-sailing single ships carried perishable or high-value cargoes, and the worth of the cargo would be affected if the ship waited for the next convoy. These independent vessels were well armed and crewed, and were also more inclined to oppose a privateer who attacked them than a less well-armed vessel in a convoy. Studies have shown that during the American Revolution and the War of 1812, as many as half of the British vessels sailing between the West Indies and Britain opted to sail independently. The captains of these ships knew the risks they faced, risks which were not run by the British alone. The instructions given to the captain of a New England ship from the vessel's owner in 1777 reveal some of the more elementary precautions their crews could take. 'Some advice I have to give you. Keep a good lookout from your masthead every half hour for your own safety... if any vessel should give you chase then make from her with all heart. Don't speak with any vessel on your safety if you can help it. Don't trust to no one at the danger times. Don't run after night, as night has no eye.'

During the American Revolution and again in the War of 1812 the British instituted a convoy system, where merchant vessels were escorted by Royal Navy warships, often forming convoys of over 100 ships, and sometimes exceeding 200 vessels. One port was designated as the gathering place for ships bound for a particular destination, and on a prescribed day the convoy would sail. In theory, all the vessels in the convoy were under the command of a senior naval officer, whose warship acted as the convoy flagship. In practice, it was almost impossible to instil naval discipline into the merchant crews of the convoy, and the warships spent much of their time acting as shepherds, continually exhorting their charges to keep formation and a steady speed. Most attacks on convoys were made at night, so during the hours of darkness the convoy would reduce sail and the ships would cluster as close together as possible, surrounding the flagship. Smaller warships would patrol the perimeter of the convoy.

Like the U-boats when they attacked the Atlantic convoys during the Second World War, privateers found that their chances improved if several vessels attacked a convoy as a

Depiction of the American merchant ship *Mount Vernon* fighting off an attack by French privateers as the vessel passed through the Straits of Gibraltar, 1799. Based on a gouache by M. F. Corne, a passenger on board the American vessel. (Peabody Museum of Salem, Massachusetts)

Observer and Jack, 29 May 1782.
**Hand-coloured engraving, dated
1784. HM Brig** *Observer* **of
12 guns captured the 16-gun
Massachusetts privateer** *Jack* **off
Halifax, Nova Scotia, after a
three-hour fight. (Hensley
Collection, Ashville, NC)**

group. Although most privateers preferred to operate independently, the introduction of convoys during the American Revolution forced them to rethink their method of operation. It became common for two or three privateers to combine for an attack on an enemy convoy, and on rare occasions as many as seven or eight privateers might operate as a unit. While some lured the guarding warships away from the convoy, others would close with it, board and capture some of the merchant ships, then escape with their prizes. Darkness or the cover of bad weather or fog helped during the approach, and the same conditions also made it harder for the convoy to maintain a tight defensive formation. If a convoy became strung out during rough weather, it became particularly vulnerable to attack.

The chase

A look-out in the mast of a typical privateering schooner of the period could expect to see about 15 miles in good visibility, placing him in the centre of a 30-mile circle of visible sea. Look-outs were encouraged to maintain a sharp watch by financial reward, typically a £100 bonus in British ships. Once a prey was sighted, the privateer would give chase.

By sailing on a parallel course to the prey, the privateer could determine quite quickly if he was faster than the other vessel. If the privateer was to windward (i.e. upwind) of the merchantman, and was a faster ship, it could afford to make a series of tacks towards the enemy, getting progressively closer each time. If the enemy was to leeward (i.e. downwind), it could sail away more easily, meaning a longer chase, but the faster ship would eventually overhaul the slower one. The need for speed in a privateering vessel is evident. A privateer usually had a larger crew than a merchantman, so if there was little or no wind, one option was to 'man the sweeps'. This meant fixing oars through oar-ports in the side of the privateer's hull. Not many vessels were equipped in this style, but those that were had an advantage over any opponent in light airs. Another option was to tow the privateer after the enemy vessel, and although the enemy could adopt the same stratagem, the vessel with the larger crew would have an advantage over his adversary.

In most cases the privateer was a faster and more manoeuvrable ship than the merchant ship it was chasing, and was able to sail closer to the wind, and carry more sail. By manoeuvring onto the windward side of the enemy, the privateer gained an advantage, being able to react more readily to any change of course made by his opponent. In a strong breeze, it also meant that both ships would heel over, with the leeward ship exposing more of its hull to the enemy than its rival.

The best circumstances for an attack were during darkness or restricted visibility, when the enemy would be sighted at close quarters. Privateers also preferred to operate in areas where they could surprise an enemy, lurking behind a land mass or an island. Another method was to pretend to be a friendly ship. A sensible merchant captain in hostile waters would run from any approaching sail, but often the prey could be fooled to delay fleeing until it was too late. A privateering captain would often go to great lengths to disguise his ship by hanging strips of painted canvas over his sides to cover the gunports, carrying old and patched sails to make his ship seem less threatening, or even towing barrels to make his ship seem slower than it really was. Once an enemy was lured to within gun range of a privateer, the guns would be run out, and a shot fired over the bows of the merchant vessel. In most cases the victim realised that resistance would only lead to an unnecessary loss of life, and they surrendered. Sometimes, fake guns (called 'quakers') were used, fashioned from logs shaped to represent guns. Faced with overwhelming firepower, an enemy ship would be extremely likely to surrender rather than fight. If they still offered resistance, the privateer would try to board the enemy.

Boarding

When a privateer was left with no option but to attack the enemy vessel, the captain had the option of either using gunfire or trying to board the enemy. The advantage of boarding was that there was less risk that the enemy ship or its cargo would be damaged in the fighting, therefore maintaining its value. Privateering was a matter of profit or loss, and if the enemy looked too powerful, the privateering captain would leave him well alone. He weighed up the risks involved and made his decision according to the chance of making a profit by attacking the enemy. Methods of boarding had changed very little over the previous 200 years. Before they attacked, the privateers would have already taken their assigned battle stations. The crew were divided into two halves or 'watches' (port and starboard watches). One would man the guns, while the other prepared to board the enemy. Sand was

The *Emille*, a French privateer commanded by Robert Surcouf, attacking the English merchant vessel *Hope* in the Indian Ocean, c. 1798. Surcouf continued his success after the French Revolution, and was created a baron by Napoleon Bonaparte. (Mariners' Museum, Newport News, Virginia)

scattered on the deck to provide a firmer grip for bare feet. The boarders would be formed into small boarding parties of perhaps a dozen men, each group led by a mate, gentleman volunteer or ship's officer. Part of each watch were assigned as 'topmen', standing by to trim the sails, or to tack the ship. Some of the boarders would act as marksmen, arming themselves with muskets, hunting rifles and even swivel guns, ready to sweep the enemy decks with musketry.

The captain would try to draw alongside the enemy ship on the windward side. He would then order the wheel to be put over and the two ships would converge until they locked together. Grappling hooks would be thrown to bind the two hulls together. At that point both sides would loose a volley of musketry, trying to cut down as many of the enemy as possible. The privateer's boarding parties would then clamber over the side and onto the enemy ship, supported by gunfire from the marksmen. Before they boarded, the watch manning the guns would abandon their firearms and arm themselves with boarding weapons. There was usually a financial incentive to take part in the boarding of an enemy ship, so nobody wanted to be left behind.

Boarding weapons included the cutlass, boarding pike and boarding axe, but the seamen would also use whatever else lay to hand, such as belaying pins, gun tools, boat hooks and capstan bars. Privateers were usually well provided with boarding weapons and firearms, the weaponry being supplied by the vessel's owners. The *Liverpool Packet*, a small Canadian privateer of 1812, carried a crew of 40 men, armed with 40 cutlasses and 25 muskets. Pistols were also popular, together with blunderbusses, volley guns, muskets, carbines – anything that could fire. Both British and American gunsmiths provided boarding pistols – hand firearms that included a small bayonet for use in hand-to-hand fighting.

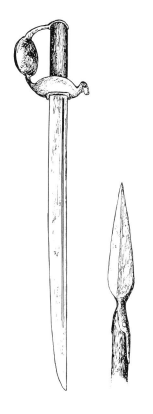

A cutlass and a boarding pike dating from the 1780s. Both are of American design, and formed the basic armament of American privateers during both the American revolution and the War of 1812. Drawing by Robert Cummings. (Author's collection)

Hand grenades and even 'stink pots' were also used, the latter being a simple form of chemical weapon, which when lit emitted a sulphurous smoke and vile stench. It was useful in discouraging resistance below deck when thrown through a hatch or gunport.

Accounts of boarding actions involving privateers are rare, the most common being the reports of defenders who either drove off their attackers or surrendered after a particularly brutal fight. These were unusual, and in most cases the defender only put up a token resistance, if they resisted at all. Action between privateers or against warships was rare, and usually only attempted if it was thought that the prize was especially valuable. They usually resorted to gunnery duels from the onset, as both vessels had a substantial crew, making boarding a risky venture. A boarding engagement could last up to ten or 15 minutes, and surrender was signalled when the officers laid down their arms, or their crew were simply overpowered by numbers. A typical example was the capture of the British ship *Pelham* by the Charleston privateer *Saucy Jack* in May 1814. The *Pelham* surrendered after a ten-minute boarding action which left 14 of her 30 crew dead or wounded, including her captain. The privateer had a crew of 50 men, giving them a substantial superiority of numbers. Often, the initial volley from the privateer would cause sufficient casualties for the recipient to surrender as soon as the privateers tried to board. Sometimes, when boarding followed a gunnery engagement using the ship's broadside, the defending ship was so disrupted by cannon fire that the defenders were too disorganised or dazed to put up much of a fight.

Gunnery

If it was unavoidable, privateers were prepared to capture an enemy ship by gunnery. A typical privateer of the American Revolutionary War was armed with 4- or 6-pdr. guns although, at least in the case of British ships, carronades were sometimes carried. Changes in gunfounding technology meant that larger calibre guns were carried towards the end of the period, so that during the War of 1812, 9-pdrs. and even 12-pdrs. were not uncommon.

They were all smooth-bored, cast-iron, muzzle-loading pieces, with all but carronades mounted on conventional four-wheeled truck carriages. Convention in British privateers and merchant ships was to paint carriages grey, while the Americans favoured red carriages. Yellow or red were both popular with the French and Spanish, although outside the regular navies of these maritime powers, no standard colour scheme existed. Carronades were mounted on slide carriages, specially designed for the weapon. The following gun sizes and weights were common to all privateers during the late 18th century.

Calibre	Length	Weight
3-pdr.	4½ ft	7 hundredweight
4-pdr.	6 ft	12½ hundredweight
6-pdr.	7 ft	17 hundredweight
9-pdr.	8½ ft	23½ hundredweight
12-pdr.	9 ft	32¾ hundredweight

From: George Smith, *An Universal Military Dictionary* (London, 1779)
(Note: A British hundredweight (cwt.) contains 112 pounds)

A naval cannon being aimed by adjusting the elevation of the piece. Much of this nicety was irrelevant on board a pitching privateer, and the introduction of gunlocks allowed guns to be fired 'on the roll'. Illustration from William Hitchinson's *Treatise on Practical Seamanship*. (London, 1787)

Ranges were difficult to gauge given the need to smash through ship timbers, but in the early 19th century the effective penetrating range for a 6-pdr. was estimated as being 280 yards. The piece had a maximum range of almost a mile (1,610 yards at 6 degrees of elevation). This was for roundshot. Shot designed to cut enemy rigging (such as chain shot or bar shot) had a shorter effective range. In order to fire grape or canister shot, the same gun needed to be within 80 yards of the enemy ship. A 12-pdr. carronade had an effective range of 200 yards. By comparison, the 18-pdr. long guns carried on many naval frigates during the War of 1812 could penetrate the hull of another frigate at around 500 yards. When ships were close enough to fire canister at each other, swivel guns mounted on the ship's rail were used to fire langrage, or 'diced shot', at the enemy crew. This anti-personnel weapon was particularly popular with privateers, as the fire of several of these little pieces could severely disrupt an enemy vessel immediately prior to boarding it.

In most gunnery engagements, with relatively equal odds, tactics and skill rather than weaponry proved decisive. In 1782 the British privateer *General Monk* (formerly the American privateer *General Washington*) met the American privateer *Hyder Ali*, carrying 16 6-pdrs. The American

A battery of carronades on an early 19th-century warship or privateer. The introduction of these lightweight guns provided even quite small vessels with a devastating short-range firepower. (Author's collection)

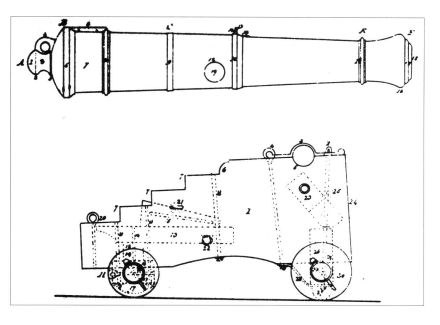

Diagram explaining the parts of a typical heavy cannon and carriage of the Napoleonic wars. Note the ring for the breeching rope on top of the cascable, and the dispart sight on top of the reinforcing ring, immediately forward of the trunnion. (Author's collection)

A swivel gun, an essential part of the armament of a privateer or pirate vessel during the 18th and early 19th centuries. Mounted on the ship's rail, they could sweep the enemy decks with a charge of musket balls or scrap metal immediately prior to boarding. (Author's collection)

crossed the bow of the British ship and the two ships were locked together. While marksmen and swivel gunners kept the British privateersmen at bay, the American captain repeatedly fired his guns into the hull of the British vessel, forcing her to strike her colours.

Later that year the captured privateer (renamed the *General Washington*) was fitted with 9-pdrs., and in an engagement with a British merchantman off the Turks and Caicos Islands, six of her guns burst, killing or wounding some of her crew. The British ship raked the American, splitting her mainmast. The *General Washington* was saved by nightfall, and she escaped in the dark. The inferior quality of some home-produced American naval guns during the American Revolution was so marked that some privateering captains preferred to use captured British pieces.

Another example, from the War of 1812, saw the American privateer *Grand Turk* ranged against a British brig called the *Acorn*, armed with 14 12-pdrs. The American vessel carried 18 pieces of the same calibre, and her crew had been operating together for almost two years. The American captain ranged alongside the British ship and forced her to strike in ten minutes, devastated by the faster American rate of fire. Ironically, the fight took place in March 1815, two months after the end of the war.

Gunnery was a last resort for the privateersmen, but if forced into a sea battle, the skill and speed of the crews were vital. Experienced privateering captains exercised their gun crews regularly, and encouraged their men to practice using boarding weapons. The best weapons of a privateer (or an early 19th-century pirate) were speed and deception – luring a victim within range before he could escape. In the event that the victim would try to fight back, privateers also had to be thoroughly versed in using their armament to its best advantage, as a quick surrender saved lives and prevented excessive damage to the prize. They also needed to know when to avoid risking a fight they had little chance of winning, such as one against a superior enemy warship. American privateering was effectively ended towards the end of the War of 1812 because they were unable to risk fighting their way through the Royal Naval blockade which sealed off the American Atlantic ports. The few privateers still at large (such as the *Grand Turk*) were also unable to return home, as no privateer was a match for a blockading British frigate or a ship-of-the-line.

PRIVATEERING VESSELS

A privateer was almost always a privately owned vessel, fitted out and armed at the owner's expense, with a specially selected crew. Its object was to capture enemy merchant shipping in time of war, not to fight enemy privateers or warships. The prime prerequisite for a privateering vessel was that she should be fast, able to catch her prey and to escape pursuers. At the beginning of any of the 18th-century or early 19th-century maritime conflicts involving America, Britain and France, purpose-built privateering vessels were a rarity, as they served no legitimate function during the long intermediate periods of peace. At the start of a conflict it was customary to fit out merchant vessels of all types as privateers, although speedy vessels were the preference. A particularly popular vessel type was the slaver, built to transfer her human cargo across the Atlantic Ocean as fast as possible. Smuggling craft were also ideal as small privateers, and these vessels were particularly common along both the British and French coasts of the English Channel. In the Americas, schooners proved ideal craft, and were usually capable of overhauling most of the other types of merchant vessels in common use. These makeshift privateers enjoyed an initial period of success until the enemy state began to arm its merchant fleet, and to send small warships to sea to intercept the privateers. The number of privateers at sea was gradually reduced as smaller and weaker vessels found their prey too well armed, and slower vessels were captured by the enemy navy. After the end of the first year of the maritime conflict, the numbers of privateers started to rise again, as specially-built vessels were launched, designed from the keel up as privateering vessels. This pattern was noticeable during the Seven Years War and the Napoleonic wars, although it was even more clearly defined during the American

Profile, deck plan and isometric reconstruction of the 20-gun American privateer *Rattlesnake*, launched in June 1781 at Salem, Massachusetts and captured by the Royal Navy in the same year. She was one of the largest privateering vessels built during the American Revolutionary War. (Mel Fisher Maritime Museum, Key West, Florida)

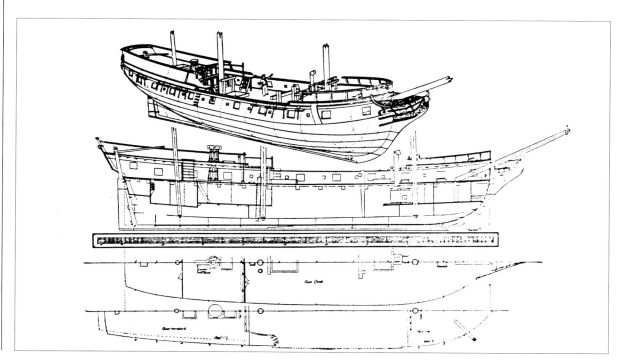

Revolutionary conflict and the War of 1812.

What were the characteristics looked for by ship owners when they commissioned a purpose-built privateer? As already noted, speed was vital, but this was a difficult attribute to guarantee when a ship was being designed. Ship designers recognised the basic correlation between a sleek hull design and a suitable spread of sail, but at least until the late 18th century they tended to copy existing fast designs rather than to produce their own evolutionary

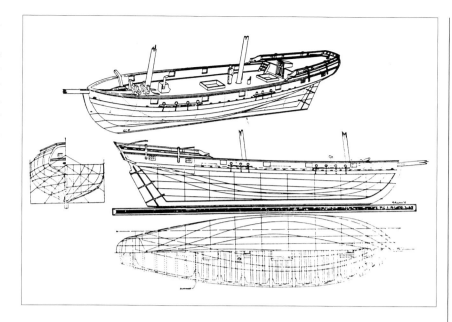

Profile, plan and isometric view of a former privateering schooner captured and purchased into the Royal Navy in 1780, when she was renamed the armed schooner *Bernice*. Although her original name and port are unknown, she was almost certainly an American vessel. (Mel Fisher Maritime Museum, Key West, Florida)

craft. A privateer had to be seaworthy, capable of cruising the enemy sea lanes regardless of the weather conditions. Crucially, she must be capable of handling well in strong breezes with more sail than was commonly carried, and able to sail as close to the wind as possible. Armament was less important, although a privateer had to have sufficient firepower to overawe any merchant ship it came across. The idea was not to fight enemy warships or well-defended merchantmen in a conventional sea battle, but to capture the enemy ship by intimidation, preferably without damaging her hull or cargo. As most privateers had a comparatively large crew compared with their mercantile opponents, boarding was the favoured recourse if the enemy chose not to surrender on demand. This large crew was required to man prize vessels as well as to ensure victory in a boarding action. Another vital feature was hull strength. The need for a slim and sleek hull which ensured speed had to be balanced with the requirement to make the frames of the ship heavy enough to withstand the pressures imposed by a larger spread of sail than would normally be carried in a similarly sized merchant vessel. As only a small broadside of ordnance was usually carried, the stresses imposed on the hull by gunfire were less than those when under a full press of sail, and the hull had to be designed accordingly, with special attention given to the strength of the masts. As it was rare for privateers to stay at sea for extended periods, there was little requirement for extensive hold space for stores and provisions, or to house the cargoes taken from an enemy vessel. The custom was to send the captured vessel back to the privateer's home port with a prize crew, so only money and particularly valuable cargoes were transferred to the privateer herself.

As for the vessels themselves, while the first wave of privateers were small, converted fishing vessels or merchantmen, many smaller vessels were retained as privateers. The French, Dutch and British all favoured small cutters, luggers and ketches in European waters. These 'corvettes' were ideally suited to coastal waters, but were unable to venture far into the Atlantic Ocean. In his *Architectura Navalis Mercatoria* of 1768, the

Swedish naval architect Frederick Chapman included plans for a privateering frigate, designed as a deep-water commerce-raider. Chapman's privateer was 160 feet long, with a beam of 47 feet and displaced 950 tons. She was armed with 40 guns (6- and 28-pdrs. in two decks), and carried a crew of 400 men. As most privateers of the day were less than 85 feet long, with a displacement of 120 tons, this was a significant departure from the privateers of the period. Although never as large as Chapman's frigate, some French privateers of the French Revolutionary War exceeded 500 tons, and during the War of 1812, American shipyards produced a range of 'super-privateers'. The ground for these specialist vessels had been laid even earlier. Several large and specially-built privateers were captured by the Royal Navy during the American Revolution, and brought into service. The process involved completing a detailed survey of the ship, and plans were made of the vessel. These provide a useful insight into American privateering design during the late 18th century.

In 1778 the British captured the privateer *American Tartar*. She was 115 feet long, and carried 20 guns. This was a revelation, as the privateer was larger than anything the Royal Navy had encountered before. In 1781 the American privateer *Rattlesnake* was captured and used by the Royal Navy. She was a miniature version of the ship designed by Chapman. It appears she was built in Salem, and carried 20 guns and a crew of 85 men. She was probably built by John Peck of Boston, who reputedly had never heard of Chapman. The *Rattlesnake* was therefore a pure American design, intended to fill the perceived need of an ideal privateering vessel. A smaller privateer for which plans exist was the *Bernice*, used by the Royal Navy as an armed schooner. It was clearly capable of great speed, and is similar in its lines to later Baltimore and Chesapeake schooners.

During the War of 1812, American designers built even larger privateers, such as the *Prince de Neufchâtel*. She was built in New York, but followed the designs of contemporary French privateers. At about 130 feet long, she carried 18 guns, mostly carronades, with long 18-pdrs. as bow chasers. This 'super-privateer' had a spectacular career, capturing numerous British prizes and fighting off a British boarding attempt before finally being captured in December 1814. American maritime historians have described the vessel as the pinnacle of privateering design, combining

(continued on page 43)

The American 'super-privateer' *Prince de Neufchâtel* portrayed during its chase by Royal Naval warships in 1813. The schooner was built in New York but used the French port of Cherbourg as her base. She was eventually captured off Nantucket Shoals in October 1814. Line drawing by Henry Rusk. (Author's collection)

EARLY REVOLUTIONARY WAR PRIVATEERS
OFF THE COAST OF RHODE ISLAND, 1775

A

JOHN PAUL JONES RAIDING THE EARL OF SELKIRIK'S HOUSE, 1778

B

LEVI BARLOW'S PRIVATEERS ATTACKED BY LOYALISTS ON NANTUCKET, 1782

C

ROBERT SURCOUF BOARDING A
BRITISH EAST INDIAMAN, 1796

D

THE *PRINCE DE NEUFCHÂTEL* PURSUED BY A BRITISH FRIGATE, 1814

THE GENERAL ARMSTRONG REPELLING A BRITISH ATTACK
OFF FAYAL, 1814

F

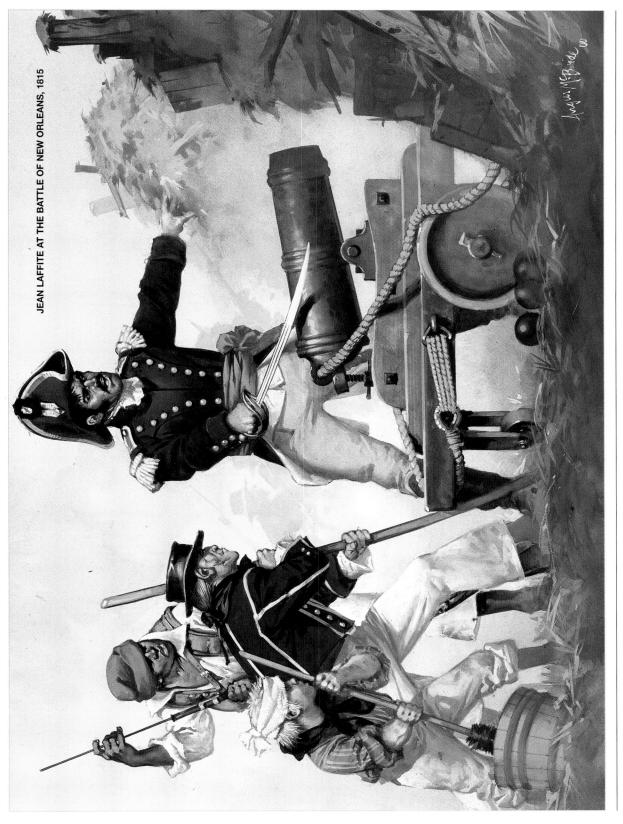

JEAN LAFFITE AT THE BATTLE OF NEW ORLEANS, 1815

G

COMMODORE PORTER AND THE 'MOSQUITO FLEET'

H

BENITO DE SOTO
IN GIBRALTAR, 1832

'DON' PEDRO GIBERT
ON THE *MEXICAN*,
1832

power, speed and superb handling qualities. In fact, she was distinctly smaller than many of the large French privateers that operated in the West Indies and Atlantic, and she was matched in size by privateering schooners from Baltimore, Salem and Boston such as the *Herald*, *America* or *Boxer*, all considered examples of 'super-privateers', or at least specialist privateering ships. The American schooners of the War of 1812 were perfectly designed for their privateering role, and their list of prizes betrays their efficiency at hunting and capturing enemy shipping. Compared with earlier vessels, they were spectacularly successful, with a combination of expert crews and ideal vessels.

American privateers during the American Revolution were painted almost exclusively using the earth-pigment paints available in the American colonies at the time. Particularly common was a brick red colour produced from iron oxide. Similarly, a yellow ochre was also readily available, as was a mid-brown Sienna, and a mid-grey lead-based paint. Of these, the three former colours appear to have been the most popular for vessels. Black, or 'lamp black', was also available, but became more common as a privateering and merchant ship colour during the early 19th century. White was rarely used, although it was popular as a land-based paint. It was relatively expensive, and at sea the colour tended to yellow and fade rapidly. Other colours, such as blues, reds and greens, were used sparingly, as the paint had to be imported from Europe, and was consequently expensive. Certain combinations appear to have been common: an ochre or sienna hull with black stripes was popular, as was a black hull with red oxide or ochre stripes. Gunports were never chequered on privateers as they were on warships during the early 19th century. These colour schemes reflected merchant practice, and allowed the privateering vessel to disguise herself as a merchantman if desired. By the War of 1812, many British and American privateers favoured black hulls with a horizontal ochre stripe down the side. Paintings depicting French privateers during the period show black hulls with white stripes or, more commonly, all black hulls.

Broadsheet commemorating the death of Captain James Mugford, who commanded the Marblehead schooner *Franklin*. In early 1775 Mugford captured the British storeship *Hope*, carrying gunpowder. The munitions were duly passed on to Washington's army. (Author's collection)

PRIVATEER CAPTAINS AND LATTER-DAY PIRATES

Of the hundreds of privateering captains of the period, the following form a representative sample, although they include some of the more successful commanders. The list also includes a naval officer and a selection of the last Caribbean pirates active during the early 19th century.

Captain Jonathan Haraden from Gloucester, Massachusetts, commanded the 14-gun privateer *General Pickering*, based in Salem. Haraden was one of the most successful of the New England captains, his most celebrated feat being the capture of the British privateer *Achilles* in June 1780. Illustration by C. Keith Wilbur. (Stackpole Books)

Captain Silas Talbot was a distinguished Rhode Island privateering captain who led his men in attacks on British warships on the Hudson River in 1776, then operated off New England against Tory shipping until he was captured in 1780. (Author's collection)

Jonathan Haraden

Period of operation: 1776–82

Jonathan Haraden was born in Gloucester, Massachusetts, in 1745, but moved to Salem as a child. He served his apprenticeship at sea, and when the American colonies revolted in 1775 he was a natural choice as a privateer. In 1776 he was appointed first lieutenant on the privateering schooner *Tyrannicide*, commanded by Captain Fiske of Salem. During that summer the *Tyrannicide* captured a Royal Naval cutter, a packet schooner and several merchant ships, and repeated her successes on several other cruises reaching as far afield as Bermuda. In August 1779 she was burned on the Penobscot River to avoid letting her fall into enemy hands. Haraden returned to Salem.

In the spring of 1780 he sailed as the captain of the new Salem privateer *General Pickering*, a 180-ton schooner armed with 14 6-pdrs., and carrying a crew of 45 men. Haraden planned to make the Spanish port of Bilbao his base, and sailed with a cargo of West Indies sugar to help pay for supplies in Europe. During the voyage he was attacked by a British cutter, which he fought off, and in the Bay of Biscay he came upon the British privateering brig *Golden Eagle*. It was night, and both vessels were taken by surprise, and could hardly see each other. Haraden called on the British captain to surrender, claiming he was 'a United States frigate of the heaviest class'. The British privateers surrendered, only to find that the *General Pickering* was no more powerful than their own ship.

When he was approaching Bilbao with his prize on 4 June, Haraden was attacked by the large British privateer *Achilles*, of 40 guns. The British recaptured Haraden's prize, and as spectators watched from the shore the two privateers fought for three hours, before the *Achilles* gave up the contest and sailed away with the *Golden Eagle* as a consolation prize. Haraden's ship limped into Bilbao. Haraden returned to Salem in the autumn and continued his activities, capturing dozens of British vessels off the New York coast. Haraden won a reputation for deception and bluff, and by the end of the war had amassed a hard-won fortune in prize money.

Silas Talbot

Period of operation: 1775–81

Born into a poor family in Dighton, Massachusetts, Silas Talbot went to sea as a boy, and by 1772 appears as a house-owner and sea captain in Providence, Rhode Island. In 1775 he joined a Rhode Island infantry regiment as a captain, and served in the operations around Boston which culminated in the British withdrawal from the city in March 1776. In New London, he met Captain Esek Hopkins, and offered to help guide his Continental Navy ships to a secure haven in Providence, he then rejoined the Continental Army outside New York. The British captured the city in a brilliantly-fought campaign, and forced Washington to retreat up the Hudson River. A plan was laid to attack the British fleet anchored off the city, and Talbot offered to help. The fireship attack was a failure, and Talbot was badly injured. He returned to Providence to recuperate, and then in 1778 the newly-promoted Colonel Talbot assisted in another failure, a French attack on Newport, Rhode Island.

Turning his back on regular service, Talbot fitted out a small privateering schooner called the *Hawk*, with two guns and 60 crew. He captured the British blockading vessel *Pigot*, then set out in search of larger prey. He captured several British merchantmen during 1779, as well as two loyalist privateers, including the powerful Newport brig *King George*. While still officially serving in Washington's army, Colonel Talbot had become a successful privateer.

His privateering sloop *Argo* of 100 tons carried a respectable 12 6-pdrs. and a crew of 60 men, all 'ex-army' seamen, and in 1779 he began a fresh cruise, operating off Long Island, Nantucket and Cape Cod. He sent scores of prizes into New Bedford, Massachusetts, including two more privateers, the *Dragon* of 14 guns and the *Hannah*, also of 14 guns, including 12-pdrs. For his achievements he was made a captain in the Continental Navy. In 1780 he took command of the privateer *General Washington*, carrying 20 6-pdrs. and a crew of 120 men. After a few successes, he ran into a British fleet and was captured. He was released from prison in Britain in 1781, and eventually returned to Providence. After the war he continued in naval service and even commanded the frigate USS *Constitution* during the Quasi-War with France.

John Paul Jones

Period of operation: 1775–81

Born John Paul in south-west Scotland in 1747, he sailed to Virginia in 1760 to join his elder brother. He became a seaman, and within seven years had become the captain of a West Indies merchantman. Some unrecorded incident prompted him to change his identity, adding Jones to his name. In 1775 John Paul Jones was commissioned as a lieutenant in the Continental Navy, and commanded a number of ships. In early 1778 he sailed for Brest, with orders to use the French port as a base for commerce raiding.

By April 1778 he was attacking shipping in the Irish Sea, then landed at Whitehaven, where he destroyed a small fort and burned the ships in port. Slipping away, he made his next appearance on the Scottish coast near Kirkudbright, where he tried to kidnap the Earl of Selkirk from his home. The Earl was away, so Jones took the family silver instead. This was considered an act of piracy by the British public, and he was demonised in the British newspapers. He then captured the 20-gun British brig *Drake* before returning to Brest.

John Paul Jones (1747–92), the captain of the Continental Navy who operated more as a privateer than a naval commander. His landings in northern England and southern Scotland made him a pirate in the eyes of the British. (Author's collection)

A portrayal of the probably fictitious incident where John Paul Jones shot a sailor under his command when the man wanted to surrender during the battle between the *Bonhomme Richard* and the *Serapis*, September 1779. (Author's collection)

45

LEFT **The action between the *Bonhomme Richard* and the *Serapis*, 1779. This engraving of the boarding action echoes the brutality of mêlée aboard ship, and has been attributed to maritime illustrator Howard Chapelle, *c.* 1930. (Author's collection)**

RIGHT **Another depiction of John Paul Jones, from the medal presented to him by Congress after the *Bonhomme Richard* – *Serapis* engagement. Jones is shown wearing the uniform of a full captain in the Continental Navy, while the reverse of the medal depicts the sea fight. (Author's collection)**

Jones was rewarded with a new command, a converted French Indiaman renamed *Bonhomme Richard*. In August he put to sea in company with French privateers and captured three British ships off Ireland. By September he was in the North Sea, but became separated from all but one of the French vessels. Bad weather forced him to abandon a raid on Leith near Edinburgh, and he continued to cruise down the coast. On 23 September 1779 he encountered a British convoy off Flamborough Head. Jones attacked the escort, the 50-gun *Serapis*, while his consort engaged a British sloop. Jones resolved to fight the British ship at close quarters, and the ships exchanged broadsides at point-blank range. When asked to surrender, he replied with the now famous line, 'I have not yet begun to fight'. American musket fire swept the British decks, and Jones eventually boarded the enemy, forcing it to strike. Both ships were severely damaged, and the *Bonhomme Richard* eventually sank, leaving Jones to limp away in his prize.

In France Jones was regarded as a hero, and he went on to serve in the Russian navy before dying in 1792. Today he is regarded as the father of the United States Navy.

Robert Surcouf
Period of operation: 1794–1810
The French Revolutionary War began in 1793, and while the French fleet found itself blockaded in the ports of Brest and Toulon, other harbours became centres of privateering activity. As the Royal Navy also maintained a powerful presence in the West Indies, larger French privateers opted to cruise in the less heavily defended waters of the Indian Ocean. The most successful of these privateer captains was Robert Surcouf, who originated in the privateering port of St Malo, in Brittany.

He began his career at 13, when he ran away to sea. He worked through the ranks, and when the French revolution began he was the captain of a French slave ship, operating between the colony of the Île de France (Mauritius) and the East African coast. When the French revolutionaries outlawed the slave trade in 1795, Surcouf looked elsewhere for employment. His ship was ideally suited for privateering, and Mauritius lay astride the British sea lane from India to Europe via the Cape of Good Hope. The governor of the island denied him a letter of marque, probably because he was unable to raise enough of a bond. Undeterred, Surcouf re-armed his small slaving brig *Emille* and went in search of prey.

One of his first successes was the capture of the *Triton* in the Bay of Bengal, a British East Indiaman returning to London with a rich cargo. He captured several other ships, only to have them confiscated by the governor of Mauritius. Surcouf promptly sailed for France, acquired a letter of marque and returned to Mauritius to claim his prizes. He continued to harass British shipping throughout the war, and captured another valuable East Indiaman, the *Kent*, with two small privateers, the *Confiance* and the *Clarisse*.

During the Peace of Amiens he returned to France, and when war broke out again refused a commission in the regular navy and operated his privateering squadron from St Malo. In 1807 he sailed for the West Indies in the 'super-privateer' *Revenant*, and then retired after two successful cruises. Feted as a hero by the French and awarded with a barony by Napoleon, Surcouf continued to invest in privateering ventures until the end of the Napoleonic wars.

Thomas Boyle

Period of operation: 1812–15

Thomas Boyle remains one of the few privateer captains who captured a regular enemy warship. His roots are obscure, but by the start of the War of 1812 he was considered one of Baltimore's most distinguished seamen. In July 1812 he was given command of the privateering schooner *Comet*, a converted merchantman armed with 16 guns. He captured a well-armed British merchantman, carrying sugar and cotton from Surinam, which surrendered after a bitter gunnery duel. The *Comet* went on to take two more sugar carriers before returning to Baltimore in November. A British squadron moved up the Chesapeake while the *Comet* was in port, but Boyle ran through the blockade in late December and escaped with only minor damage.

By January Boyle was off Pernambuco in Brazil, and by pretending to be a Portuguese vessel he approached a small convoy of three British ships and a Portuguese escort. The Portuguese brig tried to defend the convoy, but after a lengthy fight the *Comet* captured one of the merchantmen and escaped. The Americans captured a British ship, only to be chased from the area by the frigate HMS *Surprise*. Boyle evaded the British warship and set course for the West Indies. In February 1813, he captured a merchantman off St Johns which turned out to be a straggler from a convoy. The *Comet* gave chase and captured two more stragglers before being chased off by the escorts. Boyle returned to Baltimore and was given command of the 'super-privateer' *Chasseur*. His first cruise was off the British coast, where he captured 18 ships, before returning to New York in October 1814.

In February 1815, the *Chasseur* was cruising in the Florida Straits when she encountered the Royal Naval schooner *St Lawrence*. The two ships were well matched, with 12 guns each, but the American privateer was better handled. After exchanging several broadsides the privateers eventually boarded the British warship and captured her. The *Chasseur* took her important prize back to Baltimore, only to find the war had ended.

Jean Laffite

Period of operation: 1810–20

The details of Jean Laffite's early life are vague, but he was probably born in France around 1780. By 1809 he and his brother Pierre ran a blacksmith's shop in New Orleans, which also provided a cover for a smuggling operation. From 1810 Laffite became the leader of a band of pirates and smugglers based in Barataria Bay, south of the city. For four years his men attacked Spanish shipping in the Gulf of Mexico, selling plunder and slaves to Louisiana merchants and slave traders in a series of secret auctions. In 1812 the governor of Louisiana arrested the Laffites on charges of piracy, but the brothers escaped on bail, and their activities continued largely unhindered. In 1814 a British fleet had blockaded the mouth of the Mississippi Delta. Laffite impressed the British with this ability to evade the blockade, so they decided to use the pirates to help them. In September 1814, British officers met Laffite, offering him a reward if he would help them attack New Orleans. Instead, Laffite warned the Louisiana authorities, an action that

THE LIFE OF

LAFITTE,

THE FAMOUS PIRATE OF THE GULF OF MEXICO.

Lafitte boarding the Queen East Indiaman.

With a History of the Pirates of Barrataria—and an account of their volunteering for the defence of New Orleans; and their daring intrepidity under General Jackson, during the battle of the 8th of January, 1815. For which important service they were pardoned by President Madison.

resulted in state warships locating his base and destroying it. By then, a British attack was considered imminent, and General Andrew Jackson proposed a truce with the pirates if they would help defend the city. In January 1815, a British force landed, and in the resulting battle of New Orleans the invaders were repulsed with heavy losses. Laffite and his pirates were rewarded by an official pardon from President Madison, and while many gave up piracy, the Laffite brothers ignored the offer, stole a ship and sailed to Galveston in Texas. Laffite's piracy continued until 1820, when he made the mistake of attacking American ships. The American navy sent a force which destroyed Galveston and its pirate fleet. Laffite escaped, but it is considered likely that he died in Mexico a year later.

Jean Laffite was a French-born smuggler who rose to command a pirate community located outside New Orleans in the first decade of the 19th century. In this account from a 19th-century pirate history, he is confused with Robert Surcouf, and credited with capturing an East India Company ship. (Mariners' Museum, Newport News, Virginia)

Benito de Soto

Period of operation: 1827–33

Benito de Soto was a Portuguese sailor who led a mutiny on an Argentinian slave ship in 1827. The loyal crewmen were cast adrift off the Angolan coast, and de Soto was elected leader of the mutineers, who chose to turn pirate. De Soto renamed the vessel the *Black Joke* and sailed for the Caribbean, where he sold the cargo of slaves before commencing his attacks. He concentrated on Spanish ships, killing the crews and sinking every vessel he came across. The old pirate adage 'dead men tell no tales' was evidently taken to heart.

By early 1830 the pirates were operating off the coast of Brazil, occasionally sailing into the mid-Atlantic to cruise the busy trade route between Europe and the Cape of Good Hope. His prey were ships returning from India and the Orient, laden with spices, opium or tea. On 21 February 1832, de Soto captured the barque *Morning Star*, on passage from Ceylon to England. The pirates fired into the merchantman at point-blank range, forcing the survivors to heave to. Ordering the British captain aboard the *Black Joke*, he cut him down with a cutlass, then sent his men on board the defenceless prize. After killing and raping at will, they locked the survivors below decks and the ship was scuttled. The pirates then sailed off in search of fresh prey. The prisoners escaped and kept the vessel afloat using her pumps until they were rescued by another ship early the next morning.

De Soto headed for the coast of Spain, where he sold his plunder. There his luck ran out. The *Black Joke* struck a reef near Cadiz and sank. The surviving pirates walked to Gibraltar, where they

The head of the pirate Benito de Soto, 1832, from a contemporary engraving. The pirate was hanged in Cadiz, then his head was removed and stuck on a spike overlooking the harbour. (Author's collection)

Benito de Soto and his crew of the *Black Joke* shown sailing away from their prey, the British barque *Morning Star,* in February 1832. The pirates locked the barque's crew below decks and scuttled the ship before abandoning her. (Mel Fisher Maritime Museum, Key West, Florida)

hoped to steal another ship. Instead they were recognised by one of their former victims, arrested and sent to Cadiz to stand trial. De Soto and his crew were subsequently hanged in 1833.

Pedro Gibert

Period of operation: 1832–33

In 1830 the former privateer Pedro Gibert commanded a trading schooner called the *Panda*. He decided that smuggling and illegal slave trading would prove more profitable, so from 1830 until 1832 he operated a smuggling business between Florida and Cuba, with a base on Florida's St Lucie Inlet. On 20 September 1832, he sighted the American brigantine *Mexican* in the Florida Straits. The American vessel was chased and captured in what may have been an impromptu act of piracy. Before his vessel was boarded, the captain of the *Mexican* hid his ship's paychest containing $20,000 in coins.

The pirate schooner *Panda*, commanded by perhaps the last Caribbean pirate, 'Don' Pedro Gibert. A smuggler who only committed one piratical act when he captured the American vessel *Mexican* in 1832, Gibert also became the last man to be executed for piracy in the United States. (Mariners' Museum, Newport News, Virginia)

The pirates boarded the prize, locked up the crew, then ransacked the ship. Gibert tortured the captain, forcing him to reveal the location of the chest, before returning to the *Panda* with the plunder. When asked what to do with the prisoners, Gibert told his men, 'Dead cats don't mew. You know what to do.' The pirates locked the crew below decks and set fire to the *Mexican* before sailing away. Somehow, one of the crewmen escaped and freed his companions. The crew put out the fire and limped north to New York.

The *Panda* remained in Florida waters until January 1833,.when it sailed for Africa. By March Gibert was off the West African coast hoping to find slaves, even though the trade was illegal in the area. A British warship came across the *Panda*, the schooner was boarded, and Gibert and his crew were arrested as illegal slavers. Despite an attempted escape the pirates were transported to England, where their true identity was discovered. Gibert and 11 other pirates were extradited to the United States to stand trial for piracy, and in a Boston courtroom they were identified by the crew of the *Mexican*. Pedro Gibert and three pirates were sentenced to death, the rest getting lesser sentences, and the condemned men were hanged in 1835, the last pirates to be executed in the United States of America.

PRIVATEERING PORTS AND PIRATE DENS

Privateering ports

Privateers operated under strict rules, one of which was the requirement to bring prizes back to a home port. There a marine court would decide if they were taken legally, and then put the vessels and cargo up for sale. Finally, the profits would be divided between owners and crew. Most privateers recruited their crew from their home port, the base where the vessels were built. Local ship owners and investors backed the privateering venture, and the prizes were sold there. The result was that in these centres, privateering provided a major economic boom, and the successes and failures of the privateering war had a direct influence on the economy of the port and its hinterland.

In Britain, France, Canada and the United States, certain ports developed into privateering centres during the period. Although this study concentrates on privateering in American waters, the British and French privateering structure provides a useful counterpoint to an examination of American privateering. Each country approached privateering in a different way, and achieved a range of results from their privateering expeditions. In some cases, ship owners took to privateering on an opportunistic basis, or were faced with little alternative if the war prevented their merchant shipping from freely engaging in trade. As such it provided the only alternative to the economic ruin of the port. Failure in an individual privateering venture might also bring private ruin, but failure to succeed in the privateering war could ruin the fabric of the port's economy. This was the situation faced by most American ports during the War of 1812; initial successes were reversed by a crippling blockade of her ports, and consequently their near-ruin.

America

During the American Revolution, a number of ports became established as privateering bases, principally in New England: Boston, Salem, New Haven and Bridgeport were the best examples, although Philadelphia was also prominent until its capture by the British in October 1777. In the War of 1812, Baltimore replaced Philadelphia as the largest privateering centre south of New York. New York itself served as a base for loyalist privateers during the Revolution, and in 1812 it was ranked alongside Baltimore as the major privateering port on the Atlantic seaboard. The majority of these ships were tiny, mounting less than four guns, but as most of the Canadian and British shipping within reach was unarmed, that seemed unimportant.

Privateering became an American obsession, and a Boston observer recorded in late 1776 that 'the spirit of privateering is got to the highest pitch of enthusiasm: almost every vessel from 20 tons to 400 is fitting out here'. The target of these New England privateers was initially the British and Canadian fishermen operating off the Grand Banks. As the war developed, larger vessels were able to range as far as the West Indies, or even reach British waters, from French or Spanish bases. The same level of activity was repeated during the War of 1812. In July 1812 the *Boston Globe* reported that, 'the people of the Eastern States are labouring almost night and day to fit out privateers. Two have already sailed from Salem, and ten others are getting ready for sea.'

Taking Salem as an example, the small Massachusetts port provided a base for over 158 privateers of various sizes throughout the Revolutionary War, although it seems no more than 40 were operating at any one time. Many of these were prizes captured by Salem privateers and bought by local ship owners, who turned them into privateers. During the War of 1812, Salem shipbuilders began constructing purpose-built privateers as soon as war was declared. The *America* was one of the first of these, capturing 40 prizes during four cruises. Her owner, George Crowninshield of Salem, made a profit of around $600,000, a fortune for the time. While American privateering ports underwent a

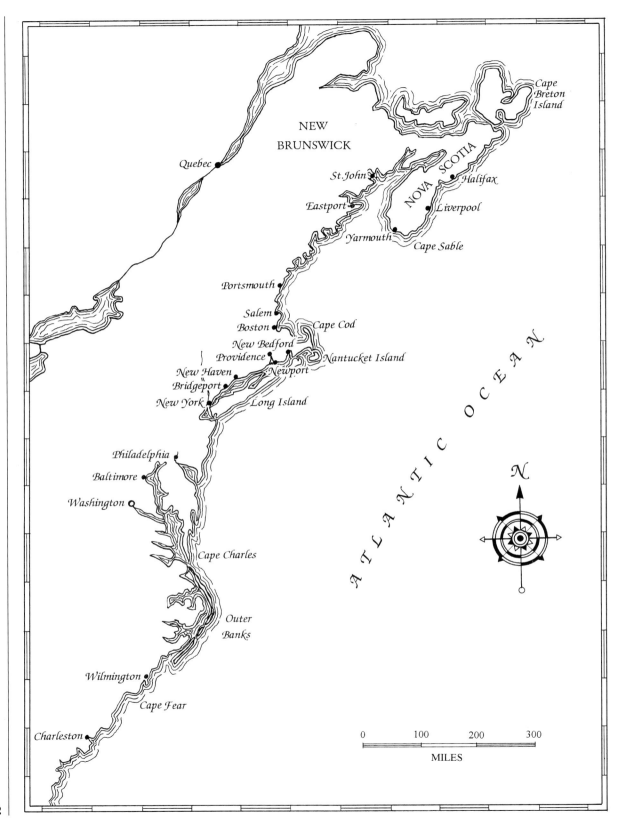

NEW BRUNSWICK

NOVA SCOTIA

Cape Breton Island

Quebec

St. John

Eastport

Halifax

Liverpool

Yarmouth

Cape Sable

Portsmouth

Salem

Boston

Cape Cod

New Bedford

Providence

Newport

Nantucket Island

New Haven

Bridgeport

New York

Long Island

Philadelphia

Baltimore

Washington

Cape Charles

Outer Banks

Wilmington

Cape Fear

Charleston

ATLANTIC OCEAN

N

0   100   200   300

MILES

Map showing the principal
American privateering ports
during the American Revolution
and the War of 1812. (Author)

boom during the American Revolution, the reverse was true during the War of 1812, especially after the full impact of the British blockade was felt. Initial success was replaced by a complete blockade of the privateering ports, and a steady loss of privateering vessels. A widespread reliance on privateering in any community imposed a strain on available local manpower and natural resources. Ships were being built, timber brought to the shipyards, and seamen and carpenters recruited to serve in the privateering venture. This was all undertaken when the country was at war, and resources were needed elsewhere. During the American Revolution, hard currency was at a premium, and the fledgling United States had no national reserves. Consequently the economy was volatile and inflation was rampant. Probably the only places where currency was brought into the country were the privateering ports. By providing a rare source of imported commodities, these ports were vital to American material and economic survival. It can even be argued that despite the blatantly profiteering nature of the enterprise, the privateers from Salem, Boston and New Haven did as much to secure America's independence from Britain as any soldier in George Washington's army. By waging an economic war, the American privateers kept their own economy alive, and subjected the British economy to pressures that made the continuance of the war unpalatable.

Britain and Canada

Canadian ports were used to harbour privateers during both wars, and Halifax, Liverpool and Yarmouth in Nova Scotia, and Eastport in New Brunswick maintained active privateering communities. In Britain, naval bases such as Portsmouth and Plymouth were often avoided, at least until after 1805, so preferred privateering ports included the Channel Islands, London, Bristol or Liverpool. American vessels were a secondary privateering target, with French shipping providing the traditional staple for British privateers. Britain was never blockaded, so both her privateers and her merchant fleet were free to operate throughout the period. Despite shipping losses through enemy privateering, British maritime commercial activity was so widespread that privateer attacks had little overall effect on the island's economy. The British privateering peak came in the last years of the American Revolutionary War, when Dutch and French prizes proved easy targets for the British. Over 800 British privateering licences were issued during the American Revolution, compared with only 175 during the War of 1812. Unlike their American opponents, most British privateers were coastal vessels, designed to capture shipping in the English Channel, not in the middle of the Atlantic.

France

The principal French privateering ports were La Rochelle, Nantes, Bayonne, St Malo and Dunkirk; privateering crews largely avoided Brest and Toulon because of the strong naval presence there. During the American Revolution, French, Spanish and Dutch ports provided bases from which American privateers could raid British territorial waters. They also provided sources for French guns and munitions. Prize agents were established in ports such as La Rochelle and Nantes, and American privateers even cruised in company with their French colleagues. During the French Revolutionary and Napoleonic wars, privateers (or 'corsairs' to the French) thrived in ports where a British blockade was incomplete

NORWAY

Shetland
Islands

Orkney
Islands

DENMARK

NORTH SEA

IRELAND

• Liverpool

BRITAIN

• Amsterdam

HOLLAND

LONDON ⊙

Vlissingen

Bristol •

• Antwerp

Portsmouth

• Dunkirk

Dartmouth

Plymouth

Cherbourg

• Dieppe

Scilly Isles

Channel Isles

⊙ PARIS

Brest ⚓ • St.Malo

FRANCE

| ⚓ Navy |

• Nantes

• La Rochelle

Bay of Biscay

• Bordeaux

0   100   200
MILES

Marseilles
•⚓ Toulon

• Bayonne

CORSICA

SPAIN

MEDITERRANEAN
SEA

or difficult to maintain due to wind and tidal conditions. Ports such as Nantes and Bayonne on the Bay of Biscay became corsair havens, supported by capital from cities where the blockade was more strictly enforced. A tight blockade of the Channel ports effectively quashed privateering in Dunkirk and St Malo after the heady period of Robert Surcouf's privateering raids into the Indian Ocean. As the Napoleonic wars progressed, economic decline within France and the increased risk of capture made privateering an enterprise that was too risky to undertake for most ship owners.

The last pirate dens

The wave of piracy that was unleashed on the Caribbean in the decade after 1815 was a direct result of the end of legitimate wartime privateering. This new wave of pirates thrived on the political instability of the Caribbean basin, and flourished in areas where government authority was lax or non-existent, or where they were able to bribe local officials. Pirates needed access to markets for the sale of their plunder, and as slaves constituted one of the most common forms of plunder, regions that supported a slave economy were particularly popular. Although the export of slaves from Africa was illegal, cities such as New Orleans provided a ready market for slavers and pirates. Pirate bases had to be remote from areas of authority, but they also needed to provide access to these marketplaces. The three following areas provided for the special needs of these last pirates.

Barataria

Barataria Bay was an inlet to the west of the Mississippi Delta, linked to the river by a network of small rivers, bayous and lagoons. It is perhaps most famous as being the base used by Jean Laffite from 1812 to 1815, but there is evidence it was used even earlier by both smugglers and pirates. Laffite used the island of Grand Terre as a base, and a nearby island contained slave pens (barracoons). Many of the pirates came from the local Cajun population, a community expert in navigating the hidden bayous of coastal Louisiana. The maze of waterways made it difficult to find the pirate base, while the same waterways provided easy access to the markets of New Orleans. Merchants and slave owners were brought to hidden meeting

The Mississippi Delta and its surrounding hinterland of bayous. Barataria, the secret island base used by Jean Laffite and his pirates, lay to the west of the main river channel and river entrance to New Orleans. (Author's collection)

55

The armed brig USS *Enterprise* sailing into action against pirates off the coast of Cuba, *c.* 1821. The vessel went on to clear pirates from the coastal ports of Texas later that same year. (Mariners' Museum, Newport News, Virginia)

places, where slaves and stolen goods were auctioned by Laffite's men, and the local Cajun population and informants within the city provided warning of any government attack on the pirate base. In 1814 a concerted effort by the US Navy led to the discovery of Barataria, and although the pirates escaped capture, their base was no longer considered a safe haven. After the establishment of military authority following the battle of New Orleans in 1815, many pirates looked elsewhere for a secure base of operations.

Galveston

Laffite and his men moved along the Gulf of Mexico to Galveston in Texas, a small settlement which for a few years became a new safe haven for pirates. Texas was a frontier region operating in a section of disputed territory beyond the authority of Texas, Mexico, the United States or Spain. Piracy thrived along the Texan coast for five years from 1815, and both Mexican and Texan traders saw Galveston as a lucrative source of contraband, including slaves, guns and more conventional cargoes. Other pirate settlements were established on Matagorda Bay and on the Sabine estuary, although Galveston became the premier pirate base in the region from 1817. All three boasted easy access to the sea, combined with safe inland escape routes through the bays, rivers and coastal waters of the Texan coast. Mexican shipping was particularly susceptible to pirate attacks, but the authorities were too concerned with the threat of a Texan rebellion to launch a punitive expedition. As American shipping losses mounted, an American naval force was sent to Galveston to deal with the pirates in 1820. The base was destroyed and the vessels either burned or captured, but pirate attacks continued. It was only in the late 1820s when a concerted anti-pirate campaign was conducted by American and British naval forces that pirate operations ended along the Texan coast. Many former pirates settled in Texas, and a number turned to privateering on behalf the fledgling state of Texas when it rebelled against Mexico in 1836.

Cuba

From 1820, the ports and inlets along the northern coast of Cuba provided a new base for pirates. Spanish colonial officials turned a blind eye to pirate attacks, and pirates such as Charles Gibbs purchased political protection at the cost of giving local authorities a share of his plunder. Particularly popular bases were the ports of Matanzas and Caibarien, as they lay astride the busy shipping lane through the Florida Straits.

From 1823 American naval forces patrolled the coast, and a diplomatic drive spearheaded by President Monroe forced the Spanish authorities to crack down on corruption and piracy. By 1824 the threat was passed, and with their vessels destroyed, many pirates turned to banditry on Cuba itself.

THE ANTI-PIRACY CAMPAIGN OF THE 1820S

The 1820s saw a resumption of piracy which had not been experienced in American waters since the days of Blackbeard and Bartholomew Roberts a century earlier. The end of the War of 1812 (in 1815) and the Latin American Wars of Independence (1810–25) meant that the waters of the Caribbean were full of privateers, not all of whom wanted to return to peaceful commerce. American shipping was particularly badly hit, and in 1823 a Baltimore newspaper estimated that there had been over 3,000 attacks on American vessels during the previous decade. Insurance companies raised their premiums to levels that surpassed those charged at the height of the British blockade in 1815, and ship owners, the press and the public all demanded action. The Royal Navy stepped up its patrols, making Jamaica a centre for its anti-piracy patrols, while Barbados served as a base for operations in the West Indies and off the coast of South America. A small American squadron was already operating in the Gulf of Mexico, and in October 1821, the USS *Enterprise* caught four pirate ships at anchor off the coast of Cuba. The schooners were the fleet of Charles Gibbs, an American privateer-turned-pirate. The pirates were either killed, captured or forced to flee ashore, although Gibbs would remain at large for a further ten years. The United States government was impressed by the action, and President Monroe ordered the establishment of an anti-piracy squadron, to be based in Key West, off the southern tip of Florida.

This US Naval force was known as the 'Mosquito Fleet', due to the small, shallow-drafted vessels used by the anti-piracy squadron. The phrase had extra meaning for the American sailors, as in the summer, malaria-carrying mosquitoes plagued the island base. The fleet consisted of 16 vessels including well-armed brigs, fast Baltimore schooners, an early paddle steamer, and even a decoy merchant ship, armed with hidden guns. The fleet commander was Commodore David Porter, a veteran of America's attack on the Barbary pirates in 1801 and the War of 1812. Porter's orders were to suppress piracy and the slave trade, protect the commerce and citizens of the United States and to transport

Commodore David Porter, commander of the American West Indies Squadron based in Key West during the late 1820s. His success ensured that the threat of piracy was removed from the Caribbean once and for all. (Key West Maritime History Society)

American specie when required. The orders given to the various commanders of the Royal Naval West Indies or Jamaica Squadrons were similar, and all three formations faced a daunting task.

The 'Mosquito Fleet' was operational by the late summer of 1822, and Porter commenced cruises off the coast of Cuba and in the Gulf of Mexico. He immediately ran into diplomatic problems, as Cuba was one of the main pirate havens but fell under the control of the Spanish Crown. The pirates proved elusive, and often their attacks were little more than crimes of opportunity, with seemingly innocent merchant vessels and fishing craft attacking passing shipping, then fleeing into Cuban ports or into the backcountry of the Florida Keys to escape retribution. Pirate attacks on shipping in Florida waters and the threat of Indian attacks on settlements forced Porter to divert precious resources to safeguard Florida's citizens, but by 1825 the Keys were protected by troops, and Porter turned his attention to Cuba. The Spanish authorities resented American or British interference, and many local officials were prepared to turn a blind eye to piracy, particularly if they were suitably rewarded. He called for a condemnation of piracy by the Spanish authorities, and cut out pirate vessels in Cuba's smaller harbours and inlets, bringing a barrage of official complaints by the Cuban administrators. Eventually, Spanish ship owners saw the benefits of Porter's actions, and lobbied the Cuban authorities to support Porter's activities. In April 1823 he defeated the infamous Cuban pirate known only as Diabolito ('Little Devil'). The pirate and his band were cornered off the northern coast of Cuba, forced to abandon their ships and flee inland. The Royal Navy had similar successes off the coast of South and Central America, and by 1824 both the British and American navies turned their attention to the Gulf of Mexico, where dozens of pirates had sought refuge in what is now Texas and northern Mexico. By 1825 hundreds of pirates had been captured, killed or forced to accept the lesson that piracy no longer paid. Piracy had virtually ceased to exist in American and Caribbean waters by the end of the year, and although a handful of rogue pirates continued to operate in the Atlantic or the Caribbean as late as the 1830s, they could be counted singly, and not in their hundreds.

BIBLIOGRAPHY

General Privateering Histories

All of these are available on both sides of the Atlantic, and are recommended reading. The works marked * are particularly informative.

David Cordingly (ed.), *Pirates: Terror on the High Seas from the Caribbean to the South China Sea* (Atlanta, GA, 1996)

W.S. Dudley (ed.), *The Naval War of 1812: A Documentary History* (Washington, DC, 1985, 2 volumes)

Jerome R. Garitee, *The Republic's Private Navy: The American privateering business as practiced by Baltimore during the War of 1812* (Middletown, CT, 1977)*

James J. Lydon, *Pirates, Privateers, Profits* (New Saddle River, NY, 1970)

Michael Palmer, *Stoddert's War: Naval Operations during the Quasi-War with France, 1798–1801* (Columbia, SC, 1987)

Marcus Rediker, *Between the Devil and the Deep-Blue Sea: Merchant Seamen, Pirates and the Anglo-American Naval World, 1700–1750* (Cambridge, 1987)*

David J. Starkey, *British Privateering Enterprise in the Eighteenth Century* (Exeter, 1990)

David J. Starkey (ed.), *Pirates and Privateers: New Perspectives on the War on Trade in the Eighteenth and Nineteenth Centuries* (Exeter, Devon, 1997)*

Carl E. Swanson, *Predators and Prizes: American Privateering and Imperial Warfare, 1739–1748* (Columbia, S.C., 1991)

The following are works that are either out of print, or contain specialised material. All are available through the inter-library loan service, or in specialist maritime libraries or bookshops.

Gardner W. Allen, *A Naval History of the American Revolution* (Boston, MA, 1913, reprinted 1970, 2 volumes)

Gardner W. Allen, *Massachusetts Privateers during the American Revolution* (Cambridge, MA, 1927)

Howard I. Chapelle, *The History of American Sailing Ships* (New York, NY, 1935, reprinted 1982)*

H. M. Chapin, *Privateering in King George's War, 1739–48* (Providence, RI, 1928)

W. B. Clark, *Ben Franklin's Privateers* (Baton Rouge, LA, 1956)

P. Crowhurst, *The French War on Trade: Privateering 1793–1815* (Aldershot, 1989)

J. L. Grummond, *The Baratarians and the Battle for New Orleans* (Baton Rouge, LA, 1961)

J. F. Jameson (ed.), *Privateering and Piracy in the Colonial Period: Illustrative Documents* (New York, NY, 1923)*

E. S. Maclay, *A History of American Privateering* (New York, 1923)

Charles W. Toth (ed.), *The American Revolution and the West Indies* (Port Washington, NY, 1975)

Vessels of the West Indies Squadron (or 'Mosquito Fleet') in action off the northern coast of Cuba, c. 1826. Many of the anti-pirate craft were small, fast schooners, similar to the vessels used by the pirates themselves. (Mariners' Museum, Newport News, Virginia)

THE PLATES

A: EARLY REVOLUTIONARY WAR PRIVATEERS OFF THE COAST OF RHODE ISLAND, 1775

Some of the earliest American privateers of the Revolutionary War were small vessels, often converted fishing boats or even sailing launches. Within months of the eruption of open revolt against the British, these vessels were granted privateering licences by the governors of the New England colonies, and were attacking British vessels owned by known loyalists and Canadian shipping sailing off the New England coast. A number of the larger vessels even ventured as far as New Brunswick and Nova Scotia.

A popular version of these small privateering craft were the launches known as 'spider boats', equipped with a single mast and sail and several pairs of oars (which gave them their distinctive name). Their crew typically consisted of around 20 privateers, armed with cutlass and musket, and the larger launches often carried small artillery pieces (4-pdrs. or swivel guns) mounted in the bow. Their preferred tactic was to approach an enemy at night while anchored in a sheltered coastal anchorage or an undefended port.

This plate shows an attack by an early spider vessel in the waters of Rhode Island, where attacks between loyalists and rebel colonists took place throughout much of the war. In these early days before a British garrison occupied Newport, the loyalists were particularly vulnerable to attack. The privateersmen are shown dressed in the standard maritime wear of the day: tarred duck trousers, woollen shirts, seamen's jackets and an assortment of headgear.

B: JOHN PAUL JONES RAIDING THE EARL OF SELKIRK'S HOUSE, 1778

Although a regular naval officer rather than a privateer, Captain John Paul Jones of the Continental Navy was ordered to use Brest in France as a base for commerce raiding in the coastal waters of the British Isles. Although legally entitled to attack shipping and even coastal batteries under the contemporary rules of war, Jones occasionally skirted the boundaries between legal and illegal behaviour. Following his attack on Whithorn in the north-east of England, Jones anchored off the Scottish coast of Dumfries, close to his birthplace. Jones led a landing party to attack the house of the Earl of Selkirk, a notable landowner in the area. Jones claimed his intention was to kidnap the nobleman, but when the Americans arrived, they found that the earl was not in residence. Jones looted the silverware from the house, ignoring the protestations of Lady Selkirk, and returned to his ship with his plunder. The British press denounced his attack as an act of piracy. Certainly when Jones returned to France he entertained sufficient doubts about the legality of his actions to return the plunder to Lady Selkirk.

Jones is depicted inside the earl's mansion, wearing the uniform of an officer in the Continental Navy. Like all regular seamen of the day, his men wear no uniform, and were indistinguishable from privateers and merchant seamen. Jones' sword is based on an example in the Naval Museum, Washington DC.

C: LEVI BARLOW'S PRIVATEERS ATTACKED BY LOYALISTS ON NANTUCKET, 1782

Captain Levi Barlow was a Massachusetts privateer captain who by 1782 had a record for both luck and skill. The population of the island of Nantucket retained loyalist sympathies throughout the war, their allegiance encouraged by the Royal Navy's use of the island as a place to buy

Depiction of the Explosion of the Dutch privateer *Dappere Patriot* on 14 August 1781 while in action against an armed British merchantman. The vessel was the only known privateer operating from The Hague during the war. (Netherlands Maritime Museum, Amsterdam, Holland)

provisions. Several loyalist merchant ships also used the island as a secure harbour in rough weather. In the spring of 1782, Barlow discovered two loyalist merchant vessels in the port, and decided to launch a 'cutting-out' expedition, an amphibious raid designed to snatch the vessels. One was anchored in the harbour, while a second was secured alongside the island's only jetty.

Barlow's men landed on the jetty from two launches, but as they came ashore they were fired on by the island's militia and the loyalist crewmen. A bitter exchange of fire resulted, and eventually Barlow and his men were forced to retreat. Barlow returned to New London and gathered together a force of several privateering vessels and their crews. He returned to Nantucket, and captured the loyalist ships. This time, the heavily outnumbered islanders offered no opposition.

Here Barlow and his men are on the jetty, trying to return the fire of the loyalists. The privateers are heavily armed, carrying French Charleville muskets converted for sea service, and a shortened version of the British India-pattern musket. The assortment of other weapons is typical of the unorthodox weaponry used at sea during the period.

D: ROBERT SURCOUF BOARDING A BRITISH EAST INDIAMAN, 1796

The French privateer Robert Surcouf spent much of the French Revolutionary wars based on the Île de France (Mauritius). The French colony lay astride the busy shipping lanes of the Indian Ocean, used by the British East India Company to transport the spices of India and the Far East to London. Surcouf was denied a letter of marque by the island's governor, but was convinced that his right to attack British shipping would be upheld by the metropolitan French authorities. He equipped the slaving brig *Emille* as a privateer, recruited a privateering crew and went to sea in defiance of the governor's wishes.

He cruised in the Bay of Bengal, hoping to intercept British shipping using the port of Bombay. Surcouf was fortunate, as one of the first ships he encountered was the East India Company ship *Triton*, returning to England with a lucrative cargo of spices. Although the Governor of Mauritius confiscated the *Triton* and her cargo, Surcouf was eventually awarded the prize and a backdated letter of marque.

Here French privateers are in the act of boarding the larger British merchant vessel. East Indiamen were well defended, and carried their own marines, making them a tough opponent. Like most privateers, the French sailors wore no uniform, and the plate shows them equipped with some of the slightly dated French weaponry which would have been available on Mauritius at the time.

E: THE *PRINCE DE NEUFCHÂTEL* PURSUED BY A BRITISH FRIGATE, 1814

The *Prince de Neufchâtel* was described by contemporary observers during the War of 1812 as 'a splendid vessel': fast, well armed and the epitome of the 'super-privateer'. Although built in New York, she was fitted out as a privateer in France. During her first cruise in 1814 she captured or sank 20 British vessels in the Irish Sea before sailing for Boston. On 11 October 1814, the privateer was off Nantucket with a captured British merchantman when it was sighted by a British frigate, HMS *Endymion*. The Americans tried to evade the British warship, and the chase lasted until nightfall. The *Prince de Neufchâtel* and its prize anchored overnight, only to be attacked by a cutting-out expedition from the British frigate. The boarders were repulsed after a bitterly contested struggle, then the privateer raised her anchor and escaped. The *Prince de Neufchâtel* and its prize evaded further British blockading ships and reached safety in Boston. She sailed again in December, and successfully ran the British blockade, only to be captured a week later by three Royal Naval frigates.

The capture of the 12-gun British armed schooner *St Lawrence* by the 16-gun Baltimore privateer *Chasseur* in the Florida Straits in February 1815. The British vessel was the former American privateer *Atlas*, which had been captured off North Carolina. (Hensley Collection, Ashville, NC)

The plate depicts the privateer during her chase by HMS *Endymion*. At one stage the wind dropped, allowing the British frigate to close with the American privateer. The French-born Captain Ordronaux is shown anxiously hoping for the wind to pick up before the enemy frigate can close within range.

F: THE *GENERAL ARMSTRONG* REPELLING A BRITISH ATTACK OFF FAYAL, 1814

The *General Armstrong*, named after the American secretary for war, was a privateering schooner built in New York in 1813. She had a successful first cruise, fighting off a larger British privateer off Surinam, and capturing several valuable prizes before returning to New York in the summer of 1814. On her second cruise she was commanded by Captain Samuel Reid, who slipped through the British blockade into the Atlantic on 9 September 1814. By late September the privateer had reached the neutral Portuguese port of Fayal, in the Azores. While the privateer was taking on supplies a British squadron appeared in the harbour, and although officially under Portuguese protection, Reid suspected an attack and cleared for action. An initial British reconnaissance by four small boats was driven off by gunfire, allowing the British to claim a breach of neutrality. Soon after midnight a more powerful attack was launched using 12 ship's boats armed with bow guns and 400 men. The British boats were fired on by several broadsides, and those boats which reached the American ship were soon forced to withdraw after attempting to board the *General Armstrong*. The British then sent in a brig, which battered the American with gunfire, forcing Reid to land his crew and then scuttle his ship.

This plate depicts the height of the British night attack, with the privateer crew trying to repel the boarding attempt. Neither British naval ratings nor American privateersmen wore any kind of uniform, so both sides adopted distinguishing marks to tell friend from foe during a mêlée.

G: JEAN LAFFITE AT THE BATTLE OF NEW ORLEANS, 1815

Laffite was a smuggler turned pirate who operated out of Barataria Bay, near New Orleans. His auctions of plundered goods and slaves were popular with local merchants, but not with the governor of Louisiana, who arrested him. Although

Dutch privateers based in Vlissingen (Flushing) capturing a British collier in the North Sea, October 1782. Engraving, *c.* 1783. The small ports of the Schelde estuary were difficult for the British to blockade, and provided a fertile base for privateers. (Netherlands Maritime Museum, Amsterdam, Holland)

outlawed during the War of 1812, Laffite was approached by the British to help them capture the city; he refused, then told the city authorities of the enemy plans. When General Andrew Jackson arrived to take charge of the city defences he offered a truce to the pirates in exchange for help. Laffite and his men agreed, and when the British attacked the city on 8 January 1815 the pirates helped drive them away from its eastern approaches.

Laffite and his men are manning a ship's cast-iron carronade behind the American earthworks. The Americans relied on Laffite's pirates, US Navy sailors from New England and regular army gunners to service their guns, 16 pieces including the single carronade. Note that unlike the army, his men rely on naval-style gunlocks to ignite the piece. The American fire shredded the attacking British ranks, and General Jackson thanked Laffite for his part in the victory, earning the pirates a pardon.

Laffite's appearance is based upon depictions of him in contemporary broadsheets, and his crews were described as containing 'Yankees, Portuguese, Norwegians, Frenchmen, Creoles, Seminoles and Cajuns'. Their dress is based upon figures from period representations of the New Orleans waterfront.

H: COMMODORE PORTER AND THE 'MOSQUITO FLEET'

In the decade following 1815, a fresh outburst of piracy plagued the waters of the Caribbean and the Gulf of Mexico. By 1822 ship owners and newspapers were demanding action, and 'death to the pirates' became a rallying cry. In 1823, President Monroe despatched an experience D naval officer to command his anti-piracy squadron, based in Key West, Florida. At 43, Commodore David Porter USN was a veteran of the war against the Barbary pirates (1801) and the War of 1812 against the British, and had earned a reputation as an aggressive commander. His West Indies Squadron was nicknamed the 'Mosquito Fleet', as it consisted exclusively of small, shallow-draught vessels. It also represented the largest peacetime deployment of American ships that had yet been assembled by the young country.

Porter is shown embarking on a launch in Key West harbour to conduct a Sunday inspection of his ships at anchor. He wears the full dress uniform of an United States Naval commodore, while his men are similarly dressed in their best uniforms. The uniforms worn by the regular navy during the War of 1812 were similar to these, and (apart from those of the officers) resemble those of British naval ratings. Of the vessels lying at anchor, one is a paddlewheel steamer, a rarity in 1823. Porter used it to good effect, towing barges full of marines and sailors up Cuban rivers and estuaries in search of pirate bases.

I: BENITO DE SOTO IN GIBRALTAR, 1832

De Soto was a Portuguese mutineer who was elected a pirate captain by his fellow crewmen in 1827. For five years he cruised in the waters of the southern Caribbean, off the coast of Brazil and in the South Atlantic in search of prizes. Although he preferred attacking Spanish prizes, he soon turned his attention to any victim he could find. In order to avoid leaving people who could testify against him, he always murdered his victims and sank their ships.

In February 1832, de Soto and his ship the *Black Joke* captured the British *Morning Star* in mid-Atlantic. His men ransacked the ship, then locked the victims below decks and scuttled the ship. This time the crew escaped and kept their vessel afloat until they were rescued. De Soto ran aground off southern Spain in the summer of 1832, and he and his crew went to Gibraltar, hoping to steal another ship. He was

Engagement between the American privateering schooner *Saratoga* and the British privateer *Rachel*, 9 December 1812. The New York vessel captured the smaller Greenock privateer after a vicious boarding action. (Hensley Collection, Ashville, NC)

recognised by one of his victims, arrested, and later hanged, along with his crew.

This plate depicts the moment of discovery. The passengers on the *Morning Star* included wounded soldiers being sent home to Britain from India. The invalids were taken to Gibraltar to recuperate, and it was one of these soldiers who recognised de Soto in the street. After he was hanged, the pirate's head was severed, and this representation of de Soto is based on a lithograph portraying his severed head on a pike in Cadiz!

J: 'DON' PEDRO GIBERT ON THE *MEXICAN*, 1832

Pedro Gibert was a smuggler who operated between his base on the east coast of Florida and the northern coast of Cuba. On 20 September 1832, he sighted the Massachusetts American vessel *Mexican* heading west through the Florida Straits, and decided to attack it. He captured the *Mexican* after a lengthy chase, in what was probably an opportunist act of piracy. After ransacking the ship the pirates found little of value, as their victim was empty of cargo. Before he was boarded, the captain of the *Mexican* hid his paychest, which contained over $20,000 in silver coins. Gibert tortured the captain and crew until they revealed where they had hidden the chest. They were then locked below decks, and the vessel set on fire and abandoned. Once the pirates had gone, one of the crewmen escaped, released the others and put out the fire. The survivors lived to testify against Gibert and his men in a Boston court, and in 1835 the self-styled 'Don' Pedro became the last man to be hanged for piracy in the United States.

Pedro Gibert is depicted returning to his ship, *Panda,* after setting the *Mexican* on fire, and the plate is based on a contemporary maritime print of the incident. Gibert and his crew are shown wearing the standard dress of Latin American sailors or privateers of the early 19th century, and their appearance would therefore be representative of many of the pirates encountered by the anti-piracy squadrons of Britain and America.

INDEX

COMPANION SERIES FROM OSPREY

MEN-AT-ARMS
An unrivalled source of information on the organisation, uniforms and equipment of the world's fighting men, past and present. The series covers hundreds of subjects spanning 5,000 years of history. Each 48-page book includes concise texts packed with specific information, some 40 photos, maps and diagrams, and eight colour plates of uniformed figures.

WARRIOR
Definitive analysis of the appearance, weapons, equipment, tactics, character and conditions of service of the individual fighting man throughout history. Each 64-page book includes full-colour uniform studies in close detail, and sectional artwork of the soldier's equipment.

ORDER OF BATTLE
The most detailed information ever published on the units which fought history's great battles. Each 96-page book contains comprehensive organisation diagrams supported by ultra-detailed colour maps. Each title also includes a large fold-out base map.

CAMPAIGN
Concise, authoritative accounts of history's decisive military encounters. Each 96-page book contains over 90 illustrations including maps, orders of battle, colour plates, and three-dimensional battle maps.

NEW VANGUARD
Comprehensive histories of the design, development and operational use of the world's armoured vehicles and artillery. Each 48-page book contains eight pages of full-colour artwork including a detailed cutaway.

AIRCRAFT OF THE ACES
Focuses exclusively on the elite pilots of major air campaigns, and includes unique interviews with surviving aces sourced specifically for each volume. Each 96-page volume contains up to 40 specially commissioned artworks, unit listings, new scale plans and the best archival photography available.

COMBAT AIRCRAFT
Technical information from the world's leading aviation writers on the century's most significant military aircraft. Each 96-page volume contains up to 40 specially commissioned artworks, unit listings, new scale plans and the best archival photography available.